Red Top

Being a Reporter: Ethically, Legally and with Panache

By Bill Coles

Paperbooks Ltd, 2 London Wall Buildings, London EC2M 5UU
info@legend-paperbooks.co.uk www.legendpress.co.uk

ISBN 978-1-9093957-7-0

Set in Times
Printed by CPI Group (UK) Ltd, Croydon, CR0 4YY

Cover design by Gudrun Jobst www.yotedesign.com

Illustrations by Giles Pilbrow

Acknowledgements

When I first started out in journalism 25 years ago, as a trainee on the *Wilts and Gloucestershire Standard*, I must have been one of the most inept reporters ever to have set foot in a newsroom. In those days, all you needed to get on a paper was chutzpah and tenacity; I had not had one single minute's worth of training.

I still cringe at the first story I had to write up. It was a story about Fairford Town Council - only I had managed to call the Fairford worthies not "councillors" but "counsellors".

The head of news, Bill Charlton, scanned the copy over my shoulder. "Oh God," he said, as it suddenly dawned on him the size of the task ahead of him. It was some task.

Although I did eventually go on a journalism course at Harlow Tertiary College, most of what I know about being a reporter has come from the mad-masters and the colleagues who took the time to sit me down and explain the principles of our craft.

I'd like to acknowledge that large debt with a heartfelt thank you!

On my first paper, the *Wilts and Glos*: my editor Anne Hayes, Bill Charlton, Katie Jarvis and the eternally patient news editor Gerry Stribling; and also Richard Martin who for ever egged me on to greater excesses until I earned my first front-page apology.

On the *Cambridge Evening News*: Bob Satchwell, Peter Wells, Chris Elliott and John Conlon.

The World Entertainment News Network with its febrile, despotic owner Jonathan Ashby.

And then, finally, *The Sun* newspaper, where, after six years as a reporter, I suddenly realised that I was still in the very foothills of news-gathering. I'd like to thank John Kay, Trevor Kavanagh, Wayne Francis, Caroline Graham, Stuart Higgins, Neil Wallis, David Yelland, Robin Bowman, Simon Parry and Sue Thompson. What a formidable team!

There were also various rival hacks who gave me a sharp little lesson in the Dark Arts - not least Alison Boshoff, David Sapsted, Andy Lines, Nick Hopkins, Tunku Varadarajan, Geoff Stead, Charlie Bain, Richard Kay, Seb Hamilton, Henry Meller, Tom Newton Dunn, Andrew Butcher and Cameron Stewart.

Lastly, I'd like to thank all the people who took me in to their newsrooms as a tabloid consultant. Being a consultant is even more fun than being a reporter. We waft in, we cause the most complete mayhem, and then we waft out again. My thanks to Ingo Capraro, Makhosi Chiwashira, Elizabeth Barratt, Mathatha Tsedu, Deon Du Plessis, Peet Bothma and Lesley Cowling.

And last, but by no means least, I'd like to thank Donald Martin, who was my deputy editor on the *Cambridge Evening News*. I'd never have dreamed that 20 years later, Donald would be ushering me into his newsrooms to brainstorm with his staff. But I suppose it shouldn't have surprised me. This world of journalism is absolutely tiny - and even years afterwards, we still like to look after the good guys.

Aside from the journalists, I'd like to thank my illustrator Giles Pilbrow, who normally has much fatter fish to fry than doing cartoons for his mates. Thank you!

There have also, of course, been the many people who've tried to stiff me - sometimes rivals but more often than not, they were my colleagues. Some succeeded and some did not - but these shysters are still worth a nod, because they were responsible for those wonderfully teeth-grinding lessons which I will never forget. I wish I had the time to name them all, but anyway - thanks, chaps!

To Andy Lines - The complete reporter; and, at least outside The Sun *newsroom, the most dangerous hack I've ever been up against.*

STANDFIRST

HE was an unshaven sports jock, and he'd caught my eye almost as soon as I'd started lecturing the post-grad media students in Johannesburg.

Some of the Wits University students were keen. They were scribbling avidly into their jotters as I talked about life on a Red Top newspaper. A couple of them were tired and spent most of the lecture yawning.

But the sports jock was different. He was about twenty-three, a redhead, and he obviously spent a lot of time down in the gym. He was also an accomplished draftsman.

From the first moment that I'd opened my mouth, the sports jock had embarked upon the most elaborate doodle.

Periodically, I'd have a little glance over to see how he was getting on. He was doing just great. Towards the end of the lecture, he'd even started colouring his picture in.

After two hours, plus coffee break, I was spent. I'd given the Wits students a complete taster of what it is to be a tabloid hack.

Any questions?

Up shoots a hand.

It was my friend, the doodler.

"Hi," he says, scratching away at his chin. "Do you ever feel ashamed at what you do?"

Interesting. I'm all for asking punchy questions in a press conference.

Though usually I wait for the other hacks to have asked a few warm-up questions.

I came out swinging.

Because this is what I believe: No, I have never been ashamed by my journalism. No, I am not ashamed to be a Red Top hack. In fact, the very opposite. I'm proud to be a tabloid hack. And, just by the by, I think most Red Top hacks could wipe the floor with their broadsheet colleagues.

I don't have a particular downer on the broadsheets - apart from *The New York Times*, of which more later.

But what the Wits University lecture made me realise is how much I object to the common belief that Red Top newspapers are just sensationalist, sexist crap that are read by morons. That's particularly so since the post-Leveson witch-hunt, where those worthies from Hacked Off are looking for any excuse to stick it to the tabloids.

This little book is an attempt to redress the balance. It's about life on the Red Tops: how to conduct a proper interview; how to find exclusives; how to deal with the mad-masters, the executives; and how, actually, to go about writing a goddamn tabloid news story.

But it's *way*, way more than a manual on how to flourish in a newsroom. It also explains the very *principles* of popular journalism.

And it also happens to be packed with stories. Sensational stories. A lot of them happened to me.

But then the world of the Red Top hack does just happen to be one of the most bizarre places on the planet.

So… welcome to my world!

Bill Coles, Edinburgh. August, 2013

I'M AFRAID YOU'RE JUST NOT THICK-SKINNED ENOUGH TO BE A TABLOID JOURNALIST
CV
-PILBROW-

RIVALS...

It's October in a cold courthouse in America. By some quirk, you happen to be the only reporter in the room. It's a big case, a murder trial, and it is of much interest to your mad-masters. More to the point, you've got the whole thing to yourself. It's an exclusive.

Of course your rival hacks might try and get the story out of the court clerks and the rest, but in reality, you've pretty much cleaned up.

Except...

Except just at the very death, just as they're about to shut up shop for the day, you're joined by another reporter. You don't know this reporter that well. But what you do know is that he's working for a rival paper.

The rival reporter comes in, panting, red-faced. When you shake his hand, it's wet with sweat. He seems pleasant enough.

Stuck in traffic, he says. Been stuck in a jam for the last three hours.

And then, with a certain diffidence, he asks if you'll give him a fill-in.

So that's the question: will you share your exclusive with a reporter from a direct rival?

Well - will you?

AND HOW TO DEAL

WITH THEM...

I asked this question to two separate groups of veteran hacks in Johannesburg - first of all to a team of reporters and then, a week later, to a group of Red Top executives.

Almost to a man - and woman - they said that they'd tell the rival reporter to sling his hook. Go get himself another story.

They'd all be hanging onto their trusty exclusive.

"Are you sure?" I asked. "Is that your final answer?"

It was indeed their final answer.

Here's my view. Exclusives come and go. If you've got a really good exclusive, it'll be all over the internet and the radio even before your paper has hit the streets.

But on the other hand... the world of journalism is absolutely *tiny*. Even Fleet Street in the UK, with its 13-odd national papers, is pretty small. Within ten years, you will have come across most of the players. And those that you haven't come across, you'll have heard about.

So the question really revolves around this one point: do you want to be perceived as a team-player? As a general good guy?

Or do you want to be seen as a ball-breaker who couldn't give a toss for his rivals, who tramples them 'neath his feet and leaves them coughing and hacking in his dust?

That's not to say we're a pushover. Tabloid hacks are not in the business of handing out exclusives.

But we certainly are in the business of storing up favours for that inevitable day when it's us who's stuck in the traffic jam and who's chewing off their fingernails because we're missing the court case.

So my general principle is that we are courteous and generous to all rival reporters. And to our colleagues and to the fresh-faced interns, we go out of our way to be polite. Charming. Big-hearted.

The reasons are simple. Firstly, of course, we like it when rival reporters are in our debt.

More importantly: we never know who's going to be our next boss. And if that boss just happens to have a bit of a downer on us - say because we stiffed her ten years ago at a certain court case - then guess who will very soon be out of a job.

On the flipside. The only way to get a good solid pay rise is to get poached by a rival paper. Now suppose a rival editor is thinking of tapping you up. What's the first thing he's going to do? He'll ask around his minions, find out if you're worth having.

Still reckon it wasn't worth handing over that courtroom exclusive?

A true example. I love it. A certain political editor on a certain tabloid in a certain country. Details will have to be blurred to protect the guilty.

After years and years, Michael had finally got his dream-job. He was the political editor of a thundering Red Top; a lot of power flowing right through his fingertips.

But there had been a change of command at the top. A new editor had arrived on the scene.

Now this new editor had some history with Michael. Years back, they'd known each other on the road.

The new editor didn't want much when he took over. Didn't want very much at all. He was an easy-going chap. Just a very light hand on the tiller. Didn't want to rock the boat.

But there was one thing that he insisted on: he wanted Michael's head on a platter.

It was duly served.

Michael now languishes in the shallows and the miseries of PR.

Another example. Even better. I have lost count of the number of times that fresh freelance reporters enter a big newsroom for the first time, only to be treated like shit by the hoary old staffers.

The wizened veterans barely grunt hello. They certainly don't include the freelancers in any of the tea runs. And they won't be helping out any time soon with any glitches on the new computer system.

Guess what happens when that fresh-faced freelancer becomes a staff reporter... and then, say, an executive... and then, say, the news editor.

They don't forget. Nobody ever forgets a single person who's done them down.

Good reporters can be promoted very, very quickly on a tabloid. Guess who they'll be looking after when they've hit the jackpot, and guess who, for days on end, they'll be sending off to Croydon magistrates court...

One last example. My favourite as it happens. It pertains to me.

The original dilemma, at the start of the book, actually happened. I was that reporter in the courtroom, licking my lips over my exclusive, and Tunku was the rival who came in late, panting, desperate for a fill-in.

We had a beer. I gave him the lot. I'd lost my exclusive. Who the hell cares about exclusives, apart from our mad-masters?

A year later, I've moved on from New York. *The Sun* has sent me to, of all the Godforsaken places on earth, Westminster. This was when Tony Blair and Alastair Campbell were in their pomp. I loathed it.

Tunku, meanwhile, was flickering around New York. He moved onto *The Wall Street Journal*; *The Daily Beast*; *Newsweek*.

The years pass.

A full decade later, Tunku gets a call from a mate, an editor in South Africa. The editor, Ingo Capraro, is having problems with his Red Top. Does Tunku just happen to know of a "tabloid warrior"...

Within two months, I was on the plane out to Cape Town. Four years later, I was a consultant for every tabloid across the entire Media 24 group...

Store up the favours. Remember that in this tiny goldfish bowl that we hacks inhabit, nobody ever forgets who stiffed them.

One of the peculiar joys of our trade is that if you sit by the riverbank for long enough, you will see the rank, swollen bodies of your enemies float by.

WORLD EXCLUSIVES...

A front page world exclusive used to be the industry gold standard. It was unbeatable. It showed the rest of the hacks that they had well and truly been scooped. Scooped. Lovely word.

All change now, though. If you had a genuine world exclusive, some fellow hack will probably have hawked it on before it's even been subbed. That's the way of our world.

That's not to say that world exclusives aren't important.

Just not important as they used to be twenty years ago.

Imagine you've got the world exclusive of your dreams. It's an absolute beauty. No pictures, mind. But it's a great, great story and, surprisingly, it's all been stood up.

Now all you have to do is sweat it out for the next six hours and hope that the story doesn't drop on the Press Association wires.

Then, at about 3.30pm, you get a call from a rival reporter. Actually, you've got a bit of a crush on this reporter. They're sexy, funny. Alive. Maybe they've got a bit of a crush on you too.

After a minute of pleasant chit-chat, this rival reporter reveals that a little bird has told them that you've got a great exclusive.

Would you mind, pretty please, handing it over?

Well, would you?

AND HOW TO HANDLE THEM...

While it goes without saying that all Red Top hacks are charmers who should be cordial and pleasant in the extreme to our rivals. We love shoring up those favours! We horde 'em! But that does not in any way mean we're a pushover.

If we've got a hard-won world exclusive, then that doesn't mean we just hand it over to a sweet-talking rival.

Only a total patsy does that.

Handing over a court exclusive is one thing. But a world exclusive is quite different.

I guess it's just about respect.

However, that doesn't mean that we just politely tell the other reporter to sod off. That would be bad. It might hurt their feelings. You never know, they might soon be your boss. They might even be your lover.

No, the correct way to handle this particular phone call is to be warm and chatty, and then at the very last second say, "Oh! The boss wants me. Can I call you back?"

And of course you do make that call back, but only when the first edition has already dropped. This gives your rival reporter a small feather in her cap, as she'll know about the exclusive before the news desk.

Specialist correspondents do this all the time. If the Environment Editor has a big exclusive, he'll let his rivals know as soon as the first edition has dropped. They'll be able to cover their backs. And they owe him one.

SOME DEFINITIONS

Not that I want to get bogged down in the detail, but for the purposes of defining a Red Top, we've also got to define the other main types of paper.

First – the local papers: the provincials. They're covering all the little stories that go on within a community, from the sports fields to the magistrates courts where "spending a penny" still costs young lads more than they'd bargained for. All the agricultural show results go in, along with the car crashes, the inquests and not forgetting all the gibberish that is spouted in the parish councils. These are far and away the best training ground for a rookie reporter who aspires, one day, to start working on Fleet Street.

Fleet Street used to be where most of Britain's national papers were based. In the mornings, in the afternoons and in the evenings, the hacks would all repair to pubs like Ye Olde Cheshire Cheese and El Vino's. Not any more though. The newspapers moved out of Fleet Street long ago, to be replaced by worthy but lucrative legal firms. But the name "Fleet Street" is still a useful shorthand for describing Britain's national press. It is a broad church and it has many members.

First, there are the broadsheets: heavyweight papers bought by heavyweight people. They may have some fun bits, but they generally consider themselves to be "papers of record". They have a scatter-gun technique to news values, covering anything and everything. Readers rarely manage to get through even ten per cent of the stories.

Mid-market papers: These are a much more difficult niche to fill, and they only work successfully if the editors have a complete handle on the dreams and bugbears of their readers. The readers are primarily on the way up. They've got aspirations. They love to read stories about celebs-gone-bad. And they don't like the soap operas.

Except they do like the soap operas.

The fundamental problem with the mid-market reader is that there are many, many things that they like, but which they can't admit to liking. It might be a certain type of book or TV programme; it might be that specially illicit thrill of seeing a star getting a good mauling. They find it all rather tawdry, but boy do they love to read it. Tricky market, as I say.

And lastly, my favourite type of newspaper on earth, the tabloid: The Red Top. So named because of its red masthead at the top of the front page. It's the paper that makes no bones about it: we're writing for the masses, the blue-collar workers, and although we might be providing them with all of the news that might tickle their fancies, we are generally in the business of providing mass-market entertainment. We don't give a damn for prissy middle-class values. If our blue-collar readers are interested in something, then we're going to give it to them; and if they're still liking it, and still want more, then we'll give them a whole lot more. In fact, we're going to carry on giving them more until we've realised that they're tiring of it.

How do we know when they're tiring of a story? Well ideally the editor will have such a close monitor on the reader's pulse that she will know in an instant when a story, or a theme, is getting stale.

But there are other big clues. When the number of ring-ins or emails or letters starts to tail off...

Or when the circulation starts dipping. Our perfect Red Top editor is like a cruiserweight boxer in the ring. (Not a heavyweight, those are the broadsheet bosses, slow and cumbersome. Tabloid editors are much, much more agile.) Before she goes into the ring, our cruiserweight boxer will have a plan of action, and if the plan is working, if the other boxer is getting pulped, she'll continue with the plan. But if the plan is *not* working - if our hero cruiserweight is herself getting pummelled - then it's time to change the plan.

And one of the best indications yet of whether you're getting pulped in the ring is the circulation figures. They tell you how accurately you're punching. For every front page, you can see whether it was on target or whether it was a miss. You can see what stories are chiming with the readers and what aren't.

There is no better test of the readership's pulse than the circulation. Readership surveys are okay, but readers are more than capable of lying. They often say what's going to make them look smart. Fundamentally, a lot of readers don't really know what they want; all they know is what they *don't* want.

Stick the front pages in a file. Append the circulation figures. And within a few months, you'll know exactly the sort of front pages that your readers - and that great army of floating readers - want to buy.

PRESS CONFERENCES...

I was having a chat with a dozen senior Red Top executives in Johannesburg. Most of them had been journalists for over twenty years. They came from four papers and the amazing thing about these papers was that their readerships were all blue-collar, yet all quite different. *Sondag* was an Afrikaans Sunday for the whites; *Die Son*, also in Afrikaans, was aimed at readers of colour in the Cape; *The Daily Sun* was an English-language paper aimed right at the underbelly of the black blue-collar workers; and meanwhile the *Sunday Sun* was also aimed at the vast black readership, but with an emphasis on girls and showbiz.

There were some very senior players. We'd have our seminars on the sofas. An exchange of ideas. So much more friendly, more creative, than going into the boardroom.

Very occasionally with these executives, you would actually see the penny drop. You would see this look of revelation as, after twenty years in the trade, they discovered a new way of doing things.

The first time this really happened was when I asked them about press conferences.

"What's the point of a press conference?" I said.

They gave me some flimflam reply.

"Alright," I said. "What is the point of a press conference for a Red Top newspaper?"

They had no idea.

When it comes to press conferences, Red Top newspapers have a different agenda from the broadsheets, the mid-markets and the provincials.

We are attempting to ask the one question that causes as much havoc and mayhem as possible, for the greater glory of our newspaper.

One of South Africa's more eccentric publishers, the late Deon Du Plessis, described this technique as "throwing shit". But to my mind that is a much too simplistic way of describing what tabloid reporters are attempting to do at a press conference.

What we are primarily trying to do is ask about "the elephant in the room".

Many reporters are terrified at press conferences. They can't bring themselves to ask a single question, let alone a stinger.

But a good Red Top reporter will have done their research; will have been through the cuttings; will have decided on their plan of attack; and then will target the press conference kingpin with one of the nastiest questions they've ever heard. Now that's what we like. That's not to say that we're throwing shit at the kingpin. We're not being impertinent or discourteous. But we are most definitely trying to make them wriggle and squirm, and if they lose their rags, then so much the better.

The drill is to first of all identify yourself and then your newspaper - this is so that when it all later goes out on TV, the viewers know which ball-breaking Red Top you're from. You then have to identify the kingpin. You do not want flunkies answering the question. You have to target the main person at the event. Then, ask your question. This can take some time to craft. Have it all written down word for word. But ideally you'll have learned it off pat.

At the end of the question, and if it's appropriate, give the kingpin a little wink - just to sort of say, "what are you going to do with that one then?"

Sit back and let the fireworks commence. Very occasionally, you'll get the chance of a second question. This is brilliant. Just ask the exact same question AGAIN. Rest assured that your question will not have been answered in the first place and it will get a good laugh.

This press conference etiquette was first explained to me by Matthew Wright, a former *Sun* and *Mirror* showbiz star who had such a rare talent for asking about "The Elephant in the Room" that he now has his own chat show.

Matthew had been along to a press conference for a new telly version of the board game Cluedo. It was a sort of murder mystery game show, and in amongst the stars was the soap star, Leslie Grantham. Leslie had been one of the giants of EastEnders. He also came with a past. As a young man, he'd been jailed for murder and had spent some time in prison before mending his ways and becoming an actor...

There are a few warm up questions. Then up shoots Matthew's hand. "Matthew Wright from *The Sun*," he says. "A question for Leslie. Isn't it a bit ironic that you're now starring in a murder mystery show when you yourself were jailed for murder in the 1980s..."

Ba-ba-boom!

Grantham is white-faced with rage. His fists are shaking. There is a roaring tirade.

Matthew's only regret? "I wish he'd hit me," said Matthew. "It would have made the front page."

Press conferences can be used to irritate and enrage even the most unlikely people - even prime ministers.

In the late 1990s, Tony Blair and all the military top brass were giving a press conference on the latest bombings in Iraq.

At the same time, it just so happened that President Bill Clinton was being put through the wringer over his affair with his intern Monica Lewinsky...

I listened to a few run-of-the-mill questions. Up shoots my hand. "Bill Coles from *The Sun*," I said. "Prime Minister, isn't it a bit of a coincidence that this attack on Iraq just happens to be occurring at exactly the same time that

Bill Clinton's name is being dragged through the mud in America... "

Tony explodes. "I find it repellent," he said, "that you think that I would be ordering this attack just to... "

Later, when I returned to *The Sun*'s office in Westminster, my master Trevor Kavanagh beamed with delight. "Nice one," he said.

That is what we Red Top reporters do. We ask the very nastiest question that we can think of.

THE PHONE-HACKERS

For what it's worth, this is how the phone-hacking scandal first started.

Every Red Top newspaper in Britain occasionally has to use a private investigator. These snoops are not necessarily acting illegally, but they are capable of doing the high-tech sort of stuff that is beyond the ken of a Red Top hack.

At the most basic level, they are able to provide ex-directory numbers. This is the lifeblood of a Red Top hack. Well over half the UK population is now ex-directory, and one way or another, we hacks have to be able to get in touch with these people. I don't know how the private investigators get these numbers, though I suspect it's probably by blagging, but for this service they will usually charge upwards of £50 a pop.

At *The Sun*, I had the luck to get in tow with a young man who was so good that he was quickly poached by the news desk. He was universally known as "Secret Steve" and he was a very proficient blagger.

It soon turned out that tracking down ex-directory numbers was the very least of Steve's talents. I'm not saying *The Sun* paid for these services. But I do know that Steve and his cohorts could turn their hand to a lot of things. They could pull phone bills. They could turn number plates into names and addresses. And for a good four-figure fee, they could get their hands on medical and criminal records.

Meanwhile, our sister paper the *News of the World* also had their own little army of private investigators offering up a similar array of services.

And one day, one of the private investigators happened to offer up a brand new service: hacking into celebrities' phones. And since the whole business stinks to high hell anyway, it must have seemed like the next natural step. If you don't mind getting your stories from stars' health records, then it's only a small step to thinking that it's okay to listen to their voicemails.

But the sort of stories that the phone-hacking was producing were just pathetic. Bits of tittle-tattle about the Royals; smut about Sienna Miller's on-off relationship with Jude Law. These weren't stories, they were just meaningless drivel.

I still find it richly ironic that the story that eventually brought about the whole phone-hacking catastrophe was a few pars in the *News of the World* which said that Prince William had pulled a knee tendon during a "kids' kickabout" and that "now medics have put him on the sick list".

Frankly, I'm staggered that the *News of the World*'s executives managed to keep their secret for so long. Not only was it inevitable that it would all come out, but it was also pretty likely that once it *had* come out, the malefactors would be going to jail. Ho-hum.

What's clear though, from the sheer volume of voicemails that were hacked, is that the *News of the World* was hacking into the phones of absolutely anyone who happened to be in the news. If a person was luxuriating in their 15 minutes of fame, then it was standard procedure to trawl through their phone messages.

Call that journalism?

The thing I really can't get my head round is how boring it must have been. Day in, day out, listening to all these tens of thousands of droning messages.

I can't even be bothered to listen to the messages that have been left on my *own* voicemail.

BRIBERY…

As I write, some of my closest friends are facing a cataclysmic end to their careers after being charged with bribing public officials.

It's been a disaster.

When I worked on *The Sun*, we were paying people a lot of money for their stories. We could not have cared less who these people were, we just wanted their stories. It would not have mattered one jot if they'd been judges, prostitutes, schoolboys or Whitehall mandarins. If they were giving us stories, then we wanted to keep them on side, and since there was always plenty of money slopping around in the kitty, then it was no skin off our noses how much we paid them.

I'm afraid that with me… they actually had to add a new piece of legislation to the PCC code of conduct.

Prince William had just started at Eton College, and for two golden years I had some quite excellent contacts at the school. *Sun* readers love stories about posh schoolboys and their misdemeanours and although we couldn't print anything about Prince William or Prince Harry, we could most certainly write about the other 1,250-odd scamps in the school.

My contacts were mainly Etonians. They got paid an absolute fortune… in cash. I would meet them at one of the cafes at Waterloo Station and hand over an inch-thick wedge of £20 notes.

I never knew the boys' names. I didn't need to. I drilled the boys very hard on how not to get caught. Above all, I reminded them of Eton's unofficial school motto: "Deny, Deny, Deny".

Rather surprisingly, not a single one of the boys was ever caught or ever blabbed.

But the PCC soon put the kibosh on the whole thing. Since those halcyon days, the PCC code now specifically rules out paying money to minors.

These days, that would be very dangerous ground.

As would giving cash to civil servants or teachers or policemen.

Though I don't like the word "bribery". It has very unpleasant connotations, conjuring up an image of a grubby hack luring a public servant off the straight and narrow by wagging bags-full of money in front of their noses.

That isn't how it is. These public servants generally leak stories to the press because they're outraged at something; or they want to get one over their bosses; or they believe that some small matter should be given an airing in public.

Very rarely are they doing it for the money. Though of course the money's going to be nice, and they're certainly not going to turn it down.

But money will never have been their prime motivation. The matter of payment was only ever discussed long after the story had appeared in the paper.

So, I feel so sorry for all my old amigos who have become ensnared in Operation Elveden. For many decades, paying money to public servants was just standard practice, not just on *The Sun* but throughout Fleet Street. Though it is *The Sun*, of course, which is currently getting it in the neck for this practice, but that is a knock-on effect of the phone-hacking fiasco.

So, if we're not allowed to give public officials money any more, then how on earth can we keep them sweet?

Well… You'd never believe it, but maybe we could just do what we've only been being doing for well over the last century: taking them out for fancy meals and charming the pants off them. It's bound to be a lot more fun than just handing over great wads of money. Instead of giving them the loot, you'll be drinking it with them. What could be finer?

AND THE MORNING CONFERENCE

I absolutely detest morning conference. I had to go to a couple earlier this year and how it all came back to me: sitting there in this torpor, listening to executives droning on as my eyelids flutter and I long to fall asleep.

When I am the editor of editors, king of kings, the morning conference will be restructured.

For a kicker, all conferences will be held standing up. Fifteen minutes tops. And, above all else, everyone will have read the news list and the sports list beforehand. Who the hell wants to listen to some news editor droning on about what we've already read for ourselves?

More often than not, conference is just a little ego-massage for the editor, sitting there in all his glory, feet often up on the table, tossing out occasional pearls of wisdom. Often they're like some dinner party bore, monopolising the entire conversation - except at least with a dinner party bore, you can tell them to shut up, whereas an editor can prattle on for as long as he has breath.

The point of a news conference is about ideas. It's about kicking around ideas, brainstorming and coming up with the good original stuff that is going to fill not just the next day's papers but the next week's papers.

An exclusive story might look pretty good on the next day's front page. But an idea - a small, brilliant, perfectly formed idea - can run for weeks. Months. Years.

And it's much, much more difficult for your rival papers to steal an idea than it is for them to steal a story. Steal a story? They can do that in half an hour flat! Most British tabloids will have a team of up to six reporters working till about 3am and their main job is to rip off their rivals' best stories. But an idea… a good campaign… a good stunt. Now that's much more difficult to bandit.

EXCLUSIVES - AND HOW TO FIND THEM…

Recently, I was having a talk with a lecturer of journalism, and I asked her how she taught her eager young students to go about digging up exclusive stories.

"It's all about contacts," she said. "Contacts, contacts and more contacts."

Well thanks very much indeed, Lesley, and it's just wonderful to know, but how the hell is that going to help some greenhorn reporter who's just started working on a Red Top? Good contacts take *ages* to develop. Basically the higher they are up the tree, the longer it's going to take to develop a contact. It can take years of drinks and lunches and general schmoozing, and that's a fat lot of good if your mad-masters are yammering on at you to start delivering exclusives.

Here's one way. There are plenty of others. Of course contacts are always pretty good to have. But I reckon that with this one technique alone, you could start delivering exclusives within the week.

It's pretty damn simple.

Go through the old papers. Just pop down to the newspaper's library. Specifically, you want papers from a year ago and TEN years ago.

What you're looking to do is see whether in the last year, or last ten years, there have been any new developments. Reporters are notoriously bad at following up their own stories, which leaves the door wide open for you to do the follow-up yourself.

A lot of news stories are just the same recycled guff, with a ten per cent worth of new news on top. The new news nib is presented in the first few pars, and then the rest of the story is bulked out with what you've gleaned from the cuttings. You can get a lot of mileage from the old editions. Sit down for an hour in the library, just look through the old papers from one, two, three years ago. Keep an open mind. The bereaved mum who's started a kid's charity? What happened to her? The ex-celeb who's had a sex change? How's she getting on?

All you're doing is visiting these once fruitful trees and giving them a little shake, just to see if they've grown any new fruit of late.

And the reason, of course, why we like papers from a year ago and ten years ago is that we can start doing ANNIVERSARIES and TENTH ANNIVERSARIES (and possibly silver anniversaries if you're up for it.)

All it needs is one phone call - one single phone call! - and you can find out how the bereaved family is getting on one year later; see what's happened to the child prodigy who ran off with her teacher; discover what happened to the kid that would only eat jam sandwiches. Nice, cheap exclusives, and they're only one phone call away.

The anniversaries are more subtle. Readers, even tabloid readers, love to reminisce. They particularly love reminiscing about sporting triumphs and tragedies. If there's been some horrific accident from ten years ago, then it's time to dust down those old pictures and produce a look-back feature.

When I mentioned this idea to Terry van der Walt, a senior executive on *The Daily Sun* in South Africa, I could see this little spark dancing through his head as he recalled one of his favourite stories: two sisters who dreaded the date of August 13, because that was the day they were expecting to drop down dead. Over the years, these two terrified sisters had lost parents, siblings, nephews, nieces and probably even the family dog, and they had always died on August 13.

"You know," Terry said. "It might be worth having another look at that story."

You know Terry, you might be right. In fact, I think I might be looking at that story on every single August 12 with a possible follow-up the next day to find out if the two dears had survived "The Date From Hell"…

AND DREAMING UP EXCLUSIVES FROM THIN AIR

The real skill for a Red Top reporter is conjuring stories out of absolutely nothing. This is especially so for the Sunday Red Tops, where the hacks are under immense pressure to dream up an exclusive line on a story that may have been kicking around for four or five days.

Picture the scene: the daily hacks have been gorging themselves on the story for four days. They've stuffed themselves. How on earth can there be a single scrap left on the bone for the poor stressed-out reporters on the Sundays?

Well it's all perfectly simple.

It helps, of course, if you've got a ton of money behind you, so that you can just buy up the exclusive interview. But most times, you'll be left entirely to your own devices, with just the two phone calls a day from the neurotic news editor demanding to know about your exclusive new line.

First up, buy every single paper from today, yesterday and the day before. You cannot have too many cuttings. Go through the whole lot. Quite often you can find a line that has not been properly developed. Maybe it's just been tossed away at the end of a story.

This can be more than enough to save your bacon.

A new line to a story is very often not much more than six or seven fresh new paragraphs; it'll make a great headline, but it doesn't have to do much more. The rest of the story - as ever - will just be a repeat of all the old stuff that's already been in the papers.

If there is no new line in the papers, then you're on your own. This can be highly exhilarating. It's just down to you, your coffee, and a little bit of creative magic. It often helps to have more people working on the problem. Often you will see rival hacks in the field dreaming up a new line together. But it's not just a new line. They're also covering their own backs.

In South Africa, I remember hearing some Sunday Red Top reporter bemoaning the fact that his exclusive on poisoned dogs was already running in the dailies. It was quite a good story: all about Pretoria, dozens of dogs were dying after eating poisoned dog food. It was definitely the sort of story that people would want to be reading, and if people want to read about something, then it's a Red Top's job to deliver the goods.

"The bastards!" wailed the hack. "The vets said they'd save it for me. And now they've given it to the dailies! That's the end of my story!"

Perhaps though, if he'd had a little more ingenuity, he'd merely have continued to glide on down the mountain - an unstoppable stream that slides round all obstacles in its path.

Red Tops have a different way of looking at news. We do not necessarily report on something that's "new". We give the readers what they want. And if they're liking a story, then come what may, we're going to give them some more of that story. With a fresh spin on it.

How simple is that?

Anyway, back to the dead dogs of Pretoria.

So in the story of the poisoned dogs, there are numerous lines that spring to mind, but possibly the easiest one might be to just call up a few "top vets" to get their predictions on just how bad it's all going to get. With luck and a following wind, you'll get some leading veterinarian saying that, in a worst-case scenario, there could be up to a thousand dead dogs. Nice line. "Thousand Dogs Could Die". Could be a splash if you really worked it. And all it needed was just a little more creativity on the part of the reporter.

EXECUTIVES - AND HOW TO DEAL WITH THEM...

Make no mistake, Red Top executives can wield a lot of power and if you get on the wrong side of them, they can make your life an absolute misery.

Not that they're - necessarily - going to be in the job for long. Some might be out within the year, and that's it, "Sayonara and goodbye!" (Though we never say that to their faces - unless they're stone-cold dead - as there's no telling when they're going to be back again. As I discovered. Of which more later.) But more often than not, it's the martinets and the toadies who are going to be around for a long, long time. These are very dangerous creatures. Be wary of them. Be wary of belittling them. These people really, really know how to nurse a grievance.

My basic rule is that any person whose title includes the word "editor" - whether that's "the" editor, the managing editor, the deputy editor, the executive editor, the editor-in-chief, the news editor, the assistant news editor or the assistant features editor - needs to be thoroughly and properly schmoozed. Even lowly sub-editors need to be schmoozed; there's no telling how a spiteful whispering campaign can turn against you.

Personally, the demeanour that you're aiming for is cheerful, energetic, optimistic and - bear this in mind - RESPECTFUL. Unless you're really sure of your ground, try not to be cocky. No, what we like is a reporter who is KEEN. They've got their notebook and pen out, the better to take down every single pearl that falls from their mad-master's lips.

And more to the point, they're just lovin' it! The number of times I have seen reporters gurn away when they're put on a tough story and suck their teeth as they say, "That sounds like a really hard one boss, it's going to take ages."

Well, yes! I am fully aware of that, and was probably just about aware of that within two seconds of the orders falling from our editor's lips. But it's my job to issue the orders to the troops. And it's your job, as a reporter, to damn well suck it up with a good grace.

It's so SIMPLE! Even if you have been asked to track down the first alien from Mars, you smile, you say, "Thanks boss, great story," and you get cracking on the tale. (And then, when your boss calls up one week later, you gamely say, "Haven't found the alien, yet. But I've got a good few leads and I'm sure I'll have it soon.")

As a news editor, master of the news diary, who do you think you're going to give your best, tastiest stories to? Will it be the pain-in-the-neck misery-guts who is constantly belly-aching about how tough a story is? Or will it be the cheery reporter who always seems so perky, so chirpy, and who even carries a notebook and pen whenever you want to have a chat? Just work it out.

A very close friend of mine - again, no names, no pack-drill. Let's call him George. George had started working on a broadsheet. He was a full-time university lecturer, well used to the cut and thrust of academia. One summer holidays he was taking time off to write the leaders.

He loved it.

After about two weeks in the job, George happened to come across one of the Saturday magazine editors. Notice the word "editor" in the title. That's a clue.

They were like a couple of dogs, warily sniffing each other up and down.

"So which part of the paper are you working for?" said the magazine man.

"Ohh," says my bumptious friend. "I'm working on the leader column."

Magazine man gets in a good one, right beneath the kidneys. "Oh yes," he says. "The part of the paper that nobody reads."

Now under normal circumstances, I would recommend a self-deprecating smile before walking on by, and also perhaps marking that man's card for future reference.

Not George though. He'd cut his teeth in an Oxford College, he wasn't going to roll over for anyone. So he comes out with the most brilliant retort, "Just like your magazine!" he says.

It was sensational. Wonderful repartee.

Except he was on a national newspaper.

And he'd just offended "an editor".

Who happened to have the ear of "the" editor.

A little while down the line, the chickens came home to roost. The magazine man had been constantly drip-feeding bile into the editor's ear. He'd said George wasn't really up to the job. Soon afterwards, George was recalled from his luxurious foreign posting.

Executives don't have many perks. There they are stuck behind a desk putting in 14 hour days while the reporters are having all the fun. But one of an executive's *big* perks is that they can really screw up their underlings' lives. And, believe me, they seem to have no problem at all in waiting five, even ten years for their sweet revenge.

A lot of executives seem to have gone to the Donald Trump School of Management. Here's what Donald thinks about revenge: "If you have a shot at doing some harm to someone who has not been your friend, take it." Who would have thought that, along with property development, Donald could also have cut it as a managing editor?

One of the worst things you can do is send flippant or cheeky emails to the mad-masters. This is EXTREMELY DANGEROUS. Flippancy does not come across well in emails - and news stories too, come to that. As with all emails, you should never send anything in the heat. With all executives, take time over your emails. Pause ten minutes, perhaps even an hour, before pressing that send button. Be aware that jokes are unlikely to work well in an email.

Me?

You might not believe it, but very occasionally in my life, I have made mistakes.

This one was a beauty.

To give some background to the story: this guy had worked for *The Sun*, but then he'd embarked into the stormy seas of the freelancer.

We may, perhaps, have had a tiny, tiny bit of previous.

I may, once or twice, have technically been his boss.

Somehow he may have got the (erroneous) impression that I was a cocky git.

In my defence, all I can say is that it had never in a million years occurred to me that this man would end up being one of my mad-masters. He was a freelancer! He'd made the giant leap! Why the hell would he want to dive straight back into the Stygian hell of *The Sun* newsroom?

That, however, is just exactly what happened.

A few weeks later, we were having a robust but nonetheless light-hearted exchange of views via email. Suddenly, and I don't know quite how it happened, the banter all turned sour.

I ended up with a written warning. I still have it, to this day, a little memento of what happens when you start fooling around with the executives. So be careful, my friend, executives need to be handled with all the delicacy of a jar of nitroglycerine.

THE GREATEST JOKE EVER TO HAVE FALLEN FROM RUPERT MURDOCH'S LIPS

I don't imagine Rupert Murdoch being much of a joker. He seems like the kind of guy who is more hooked on power than cracking jokes.

Maybe I'm doing him down. Maybe Rupert is a real laugh.

Anyway – there is one joke that he is said to have quipped, and here it is. I give it to you only because it's hilarious.

Murdoch had caught a cold after running the faked-up Hitler Diaries in his *Sunday Times*. Though not much of a cold: his paper may have lost a bit of credibility, but the sales went through the roof.

Anyway – somebody had to carry the can for the Hitler fiasco, and that somebody was the *Sunday Times* editor, Frank Giles.

Frank was told that he was to be given the honorific title of "Editor Emeritus". Now that is a weird title – it's the sort of thing given to old professors when they are put out to pasture.

"Editor Emeritus?" pipes Frank. "What does that mean?"

"It's Latin, Frank," booms Murdoch. "The 'E' means you're out of here, and the 'Meritus' means you deserve it!"

ON BEING SQUEEZED

If you ever become a Red Top reporter, then let me assure you of one thing: one day, you are going to find yourself being squeezed by one of the mad-masters.

Life on a Red Top is conducted under extreme pressure. That is particularly so for the Red Tops in the UK. Reporters are being relentlessly driven by the mad-masters on the news desk. The news editors are for ever being harried and hassled by the mad-masters on the back-bench. Then, at all hours, the back-bench is being whipped by that maddest of mad-masters, the editor. And as for the editor - well they are constantly being driven onwards and upwards. One way or another, the publisher is always going to nail them. Day in, day out, they'll come under fire for low-grade stories, or blown budgets, or stagnating circulation. (And as for the Publishers, what is it that spurs them on? Perhaps it was the mad-dads who whelped them while they were still in short trousers?

Who can tell? But what I can tell you is this: a publisher's defining purpose is - or so it seems - to turn their editors' lives into a rich misery.)

The competition in Red Top papers is intense. Kind of scary yet, on the odd occasion when you deliver in an exclusive, there is nothing to touch it. The ecstasy! It sometimes lasts all of an hour.

But what I'm talking about is pressure from the bosses. Pressure, say, to bring in new and fresh exclusives. Pressure, perhaps, to start slightly tweaking with the PCC's code of conduct. Pressure, say, that makes you think it's okay to start trawling through celebs' voicemails. Not that you'd ever do it yourself. But you might, if pushed, be prepared to commission somebody else to do it for you.

More than likely, however, the pressure from the mad-masters will start very, very softly. You may have mentioned a story, which you're on the verge of writing up. Perhaps the mad-masters are desperate for a splash. Perhaps they're not. Who can ever fathom the inner workings of their minds?

Then, a mad-master will sidle up to you and will endeavour to get you to beef up the story. It might be just a new line; it might be just the slightest tweak; and sometimes, I'm afraid, it will be stretching the facts to breaking point.

What happens now is down to you. Your personal conscience. Your general hunger for exclusives. Maybe you'll trot out the line exactly as per the mad-master's orders, maybe you won't.

It's your call. Either way, I understand.

But let me promise you one thing, and it is this: if the shit hits the fan and the writs start flying and the editors start hollering, then you are totally 100 per cent on your own. Because you filed the story. You may do your level best to wriggle out of it. But ultimately if the story's got your name on it, then it's going to be you who's carrying the can. (Though once in a century it is true that, as with the *News of the World*, you may be able to bring down the whole paper with you.)

But generally, those mad-masters only got to their much-vaunted positions because they are as smart as a pack of monkeys. One thing they're very good at is dodging the flak when a story goes pear-shaped. That particularly goes for when it was them who were egging you on in the first place.

One way you can be squeezed is when a mad-master comes out with this line: "Can we say that… ?"

They'll then say something fairly far-fetched. Well if you're going to stop this train from turning into a complete runaway, you have got to do it *immediately*, because within an hour, they'll already have drawn up the front page and the back-bench will be aquiver for your copy. That train is already pelting at full-tilt down the track, and it's now going to take considerable force of will to try and stop it.

In 1988, *The Sun*'s Royal reporter, Harry Arnold, had had a strong tip that the Duchess of York was pregnant, but was still nowhere near standing the story up. He mentioned his doubts to the editor Kelvin MacKenzie, who promptly ordered him to file. "Don't worry," MacKenzie said. "Just fucking file."

Arnold laid it on thick. Reams of quotes about the thrilled families. And the next day, to Arnold's delight and utter astonishment, he saw that not one single word of his copy had been altered. He had been paid the ultimate compliment. His splash copy was exactly as he'd dictated it to the copytakers.

Only much later, when he was chatting with one of the subs, did he realise the dirty work that had occurred at the crossroads. As soon as Arnold's copy had dropped, MacKenzie had instructed the backbench: "Don't change a word of this. Then if he's got it wrong, the little fucker won't be able to wriggle out of this one!"

Nine years later and I was the New York Correspondent of *The Sun*, probably the most exciting job that a hack can have. That morning, the fashion king Gianni Versace had been gunned down on his doorstep in Miami. A huge story.

I'm all over it. From my windowless bunker on Sixth Avenue in Manhattan, I have written the nose for the story, and I've got two TVs going full blast as I send over take after take to London. On the big stories, Red Top subs can never have too much copy.

By midafternoon, the man who was in the frame for Versace's murder was a gay serial killer who'd been roaming about America. His name was Andrew Cunanan.

At about 9pm, I headed to the airport to catch the last flight down to Miami. I checked into my hotel at around 1am.

Four hours later, the phone started ringing. Of course it started ringing. It may only have been 5am, but already the mad-masters wanted to know what my exclusive splash was going to be for the next day's paper.

Hmmm. "I'll get back to you," I said.

I did what any other foreign correspondent would do. I turned on the television and bought all the papers to see if there was any fresh line that was worth filching. Nada.

By now, it's 9am. I've only got a couple of hours to file my exclusive splash. Not easy in a city that I've only been in for all of eight hours.

I went out for breakfast with a veteran freelance, Mike McDonagh. We started kicking ideas around. I learned that *one* of several theories being explored by police was that Versace had had an affair with Cunanan.

I mentioned the fact on the phone to a mad-master.

Within one minute, I'd been called right back by the maddest of the mad-masters.

"Can we say… " he said, "that Versace and Cunanan were gay lovers?"

I hedged. "Umm," I said. "That is one of the theories that is being investigated by police."

"Well we can say it then!"

With a heavy heart: "The police are considering it, yes."

"Great! File! Now!"

But as I wrote the splash, I started to perk up. I had realised that there were only two people on earth who could possibly deny the story. Of these, one was dead and the other was a serial killer on the run. Suing *The Sun* was probably not going to be high on Andrew Cunanan's list of priorities.

Into my splash was incorporated a number of caveats, phrases like "police believe" and "one of the theories being explored".

But by the time *The Sun* hit the streets, these caveats had all been stripped from the story. The front page headline read, "LOVERS" with the blunt first sentence: "Murdered fashion king Gianni Versace and the nut who shot him were once gay lovers, it was revealed last night." *

I basked in all of 30 seconds of praise from the mad-masters. The rest of the pack: monumentally shafted. They didn't seem to mind. Much.

So, that time, I'd got away with it. But if you're working on a Red Top, then you must realise that the mad-masters are going to be pressuring you constantly. Sometimes you'll cave in. Sometimes you won't. But if you *do* deliver exactly what they want, then you better be absolutely certain that you're covered. Because when it all goes pear-shaped - as it has a very great tendency to do on the Red Tops - then you will assuredly be the first in the firing line. The mad-masters may eventually be for the high jump. But that'll only happen way, *way* after you've served your prison sentence. Just ask the *News of the World*'s Royal Editor Clive Goodman. His mad-masters were only dragged down a full three years after he'd been released from prison.

* A great world exclusive splash - though I was *mightily* relieved when, two weeks later, Andrew Cunanan killed himself after being caught holed up on a houseboat in Miami.

GORE…

The Great White Hyena, Deon Du Plessis, had had a brilliant idea. He'd spotted a huge gap in the South African newspaper market. It was a few years after the end of Apartheid, and perceived wisdom held that black people did not actually read newspapers. Deon didn't think so.

He took his idea to Tony O'Reilly at Independent Newspapers and was turned down flat.

Rupert Murdoch's empire, News Corp, also gave Deon the thumbs down.

In the end, Deon ended up with the South African group Media 24 and his new paper, *The Daily Sun*, went off like an absolute rocket.

Never mind that for many black readers, English was sometimes their third language. They were gobbling it up.

The paper has a very interesting style of story-writing, I have never seen a style like it. It's almost as if you're telling a story to a child. Words of more than two syllables generally don't make it into the paper.

And one of the specialities of *The Daily Sun* was the slogan: "If it bleeds, it leads". For a long time, this was their defining mantra. It meant that if there was a particularly gory murder, then it generally led the next day's paper. And believe you me, South Africa has more than its fair share of gory murders. Every weekend, the benumbed news editors have a score of murders to choose from.

But the question is, at what stage is gore no longer really news? Well there's a pretty easy answer to that. In Red Top terms, something is only news when people are talking about it in the canteen, and if readers *aren't* talking about it in the canteen, then it is *not* news. Simple as that. So, in my book, the only murders that should be leading *The Daily Sun* are the ones that are absolutely *extraordinary*. Anything else doesn't make the cut.

That's not to say that gore should not be a regular part of the Red Top mix. For centuries now, blue-collar workers have loved reading about gore. Over 170 years ago, when the broadsheets were still as up themselves as they are today, Britain's equivalent of a Red Top newspaper was *The Penny Dreadful*. For a penny, you could have all the goriest details of the country's most hideous serial killer, Jack The Ripper. *The Penny Dreadful*'s sold in their tens of thousands; and as for Jack The Ripper, he's still as popular today as he ever was. The authors are still writing about him, and the Red Tops are *still* serialising his goriest exploits.

But what I am saying about gore is that it is just a part of the Red Top mix because though our readers may largely be working class, they have a variety of tastes. And front page after front page of gore, well it might sate them for a while. But I guess I'd give it about six or seven years before they got bored and go off to try something else.

AND BORED OF GORE

Just like today's blue-collar workers, the Romans loved their gore. Their favourite pastime was to go along to the circus to see the gladiators skewering each other to death. Can you imagine? From the comfort of your cushioned seat in the Colosseum, you could watch guys fight to the death - right there! Just a few yards in front of your very eyes! It would have knocked even the goriest *Daily Sun* front page into a cocked hat!

The circus was one of the many boons of the Emperor. If the gladiators had put on a great show, then it was the Emperor who got all the glory.

Of course the regulation fights just involved a handful of gladiators butchering each other, but every so often they'd pep things up by throwing in a few animals. Say twenty gladiators against thirty enraged lions. Who would you put your money on?

And very, very occasionally - say once a year - they'd have the big showcase fights when, right there in the Colosseum, they'd reconstruct some of Rome's greatest victories. Some two hundred gladiators dressed as legionaries would re-enact the battle of Cannae as they slaughtered two hundred barbarians. A variation on the theme was to recreate Rome's favourite pirate battles. They'd flood the Colosseum, send in the ships, and this time it would be the pirates who were hacked to bits.

The crowds loved it. The Emperor would be cheered for minutes on end. At that moment he truly must have thought himself an immortal.

One of the madder Emperors, Caligula, loved the applause so much that he decided to turn these gladiatorial battles into standard fare at the Colosseum. Instead of having the battles once a year, he put them on once a week.

For a little while, the mob loved it. Everyone loves a bit of gore.

The problem was that it was pretty difficult to top a massed battle when, only the previous week, you'd already witnessed hundreds of other gladiators get butchered.

It seems incredible, but even the Romans could get bored with gore. Despite all the hundreds of different ways that a man can die, the mob got fed up and went on the rampage. Today, fortunately, when readers get bored of gore, they just switch to another paper…

THE CARCASSES OF THE GIANTS

History is littered with the carcasses of once giant papers which have failed to adapt.

What's happened is that the publishers have initially observed some huge gap in the market and then ruthlessly exploited it. These niche markets can be immensely lucrative. You have a plan and you stick to it - whether it's giving the readers great glossy photos, or giving them front page after front page of showbiz schlock.

Or at least you stick to the plan until the circulation figures tell you to do otherwise. But so long as the circulation's going up, then of course you keep plugging away with the same routine. If the readers are clamouring for gore, or sex, then that's what you give them.

When Big Brother came out in 1999, the Editor of *The Daily Star* noticed that the circulation had a bit of a boost every time they splashed with a Big Brother story. So they did it again… and again… and again, running with a Big Brother story for the entire duration of the series. It paid big dividends.

The corollary of that view must surely be that if the circulation's going down, then it's time to try something new. To me, it seems painfully obvious. But I can tell you there are scores of editors out there who, five years back, dreamt up a brilliant strategy that saw sales soar. They imagine they've discovered "The Answer". The complete solution on how to sell a ton of papers.

And then, when sales start to take a bit of a dip, they just continue doing the same damn thing, but harder. If they've pinned their colours to showbiz, then they just hit the readers with *more* showbiz.

May I explain something? I feel almost embarrassed about having to do this, since it is so goddamn obvious. But a publisher may have carved out the most brilliant niche in the world for his brand new newspaper. He may be selling Red Tops by the million. But if he's making good money, then the only cast-iron certainty is that pretty soon some other newspaper will be stealing the idea, and possibly even doing it better.

When I was on *The Sun*, the head of promotions came up with a simply sensational idea: Sun Syndicates. It was brilliant. The lottery had just started in the UK and the scheme involved *The Sun* buying up 50,000 lottery tickets. The readers would each get five lottery lines, becoming a member of a 100-strong Sun Syndicate. Of course not much was going to happen if their lines only got four balls out of the six. But if they hit the jackpot, then every reader in the Sun Syndicate might be getting a hundredth share of £10 million.

Ingenious! The day that Sun Syndicates was launched, the Saturday sales went through the roof.

The next week... not so good. The idea had been so successful, that by the next week, the *Mirror*, *Hello!* magazine, *OK!* magazine and probably the *Beano* had all jumped on board. Everyone was playing Syndicates!

Even more galling for my editor Stuart Higgins was that although Sun syndicates went on for months, it was the *Mirror* who hit the first jackpot.

Now that must have been a choker...

You may have come up with the most sensational plan for a Red Top. But if it's making you a lot of money, then rest assured that the rest of the mob will soon be diving in with you. Come on in, Chaps, the water's warm!

So, as I warm to my theme, the only real solution for editors is to be cruiserweights; fly on their feet as they dance around the ring; adaptable; and above all else, receptive to new ideas.

Life magazine. A superb magazine. I remember loving it when I was a kid. Terrific glossy pictures of enticing people and places.

Who would have thought that other magazines and even newspapers would also be able to produce excellent pictures?

Down the swanee, I'm afraid.

And to round off, one of my all-time favourite cautionary tales. This is what happens to a newspaper if the publisher remains glued to his old and faded glories.

The *Sunday Sport* was launched with a simply remarkable newspaper concept: just make up the stories.

But if the stories were weird enough, whacky enough, outrageous enough, then people might just buy them.

I was at university the first time I came across the *Sunday Sport*, and the headline was so absurd that I laughed out loud and bought the paper: "World War II Bomber Found On Moon".

Week after week, they followed it up with even more daft front pages. These included, "Double Decker Bus Found On North Pole", and "Elvis Presley Found Hiding In Cupboard".

For a while, these headlines were quite funny. But the problem was that once you'd run with, "Hitler Was A Woman", it was going to be very difficult to top it.

By now the *Sunday Sport* was so successful that it had spawned the *Daily Sport*. Since fantasy stories were now finished, the publisher came up with another revolutionary concept: "Tits and Bums". Who would have thought it? Apparently blue-collar workers like to look at pictures of scantily clad women.

The *Sport*, however, took Tits and Bums to a breathtaking new level. Their speciality was to insist that all photographers took their shots - literally - from the gutter, aiming their cameras straight up a starlet's skirt just as she climbed out of a car. The starlet's picture, along with a titillating black star over the sauciest bit, would then be slapped all over the front page. The readers loved it!

Another variation on the theme was to track down digitally manipulated photos of stars on the internet. These photos invariably involved putting a star's head onto a beautiful nude body, and the *Sport* would then run all the photos as they claimed there'd been an outcry over this outrageous piece of computer trickery. (But *whoever* could have put those sordid pictures on the net? Beats me! I just have *no* idea!)

Anyway, I suppose all this ridiculousness worked for a while with the *Sport*. There was, however, a certain amount of amusement in the Coles household when the paper folded in April 2011. (The paper has subsequently been sold and relaunched, but it is a mere shadow of what it was in the 1980s.)

THE WORLD'S WORST

As ever, there is the occasional exception to the rule, and that would probably be my least favourite paper on earth, *The New York Times*.

I was in New York for two years with *The Sun*, and I have never come across a newspaper whose editorial staff are quite so up themselves. News stories, even really hard news stories, are invariably seen as a vehicle for *The New York Times'* brilliant reporters to show off their outstanding writing skills.

I remember having to wade through this wretched beast of a paper and time after time, I'd have to plough through about ten sentences of whimsical drivel before I got to the actual news point of the story.

You could only get away with this sort of bullshit on *The New York Times*, but that is solely because it has precisely zero competition. In New York, there are very few newspapers, and *The New York Times* is the only broadsheet of note. This means that the paper and its dinosaur staff have not had to evolve one jot. Why bother to spruce up the writing - or indeed their God-awful front page - when there's no other paper in New York for the smart middle classes to buy?

By way of contrast, just take a look at the newspaper scene in Britain. There are about twelve daily newspapers in England and in Scotland, you can choose from *eight* different broadsheets. (Want me to spell them out? I'd love to! They are: *The Telegraph, Independent, Times, Guardian, Wall Street Journal, Financial Times, Herald* and *Scotsman*.) The competition is absolutely cut-throat and the fusty old *New York Times* would be a much, much superior paper if it had even the tiniest amount of competition.

One thing, I admit, that *The New York Times* does well is getting its teeth stuck into a scandal. If there's been some sort of political cover-up, they will grind away until they eventually get their man.

But the one question I'd like to ask about *The New York Times* is this: is it actually possible for a newspaper to get any further up its own arse?

An example? I have many.

A few days after the world's most wanted man, Osama bin Laden, had been shot dead in his lair in Pakistan, *The New York Times* issued the most fantastical memo to its staff. It wasn't much. But this memo revealed absolutely everything about the values of the paper. It was the tip of the iceberg - and what an iceberg, just riddled with self-importance and over-weening vanity.

In all future stories about Osama bin Laden, the memo stated, they would be dropping the honorific, and would no longer refer to him as "Mr bin Laden".

Perhaps one day they'll stop referring to Adolf Hitler as "Mr Hitler".

IDEAS - AND HOW
TO GET THEM

Above all else on a newspaper, I love ideas. Not that there's anything wrong with all those hard-hitting exclusives. But an idea tends to start as just this little worm of light in your head and somehow, after years of diligent cultivation, you learn how to seize it.

The source material for ideas is spattering out at you most of the day: the newspapers, the magazines, the radio, the telly, the internet. But the difficulty, always, is in spotting the idea and grabbing it.

In Johannesburg, I was explaining to some editors a quirky little idea on how to prevent the readers from sharing their papers. Many of the Red Tops in South Africa are shared by up to ten people. We'd been discussing, hypothetically, about how to get the readers to buy the paper rather than borrow their mate's copy.

"What about vouchers?" I said. "We salt the paper with vouchers - on Page 2, Page 4 and the penultimate page, so that the paper ends up like a piece of confetti?"

"It's so simple!" says one executive.

Yes, my friend, it is indeed simple. But if it was so bloody simple, then how come it'd taken nearly a decade for someone to dream up the idea?

One of the slight downsides of having a brilliant idea is that once it's been explained in its entirety, it's not only going to seem simple but even glaringly obvious.

All I can say is that if these ideas are so staggeringly simple, then how come they're such a rarity?

In many newspapers, there is often an air of industry, but not really creativity. The mad-masters love their front page exclusives. Everyone loves an exclusive splash. But ideas are far more nebulous. Much more difficult to categorise and quantify.

Ideas, however, are much more difficult for other newspapers to steal and, more pertinently, they've got a much longer shelf life.

As we know, a good world exclusive is going to be old news even before it's hit the streets. Your readers will have heard it all on the radio long before they've bought the paper.

But an idea, one single idea, can run for months.

I remember when my loveliest news editor, Sue Thompson, was watching a kid staring goggle-eyed at the TV. The kid was utterly transfixed by this new TV programme, Teletubbies.

Unlike most people, Sue seized on this little germ of an idea and mentioned it to a boss at *The Sun*.

A feature was immediately turned round for the next day's paper.

At a conservative estimate, I would guess that Teletubby-fever raged across Britain for at least the next year. Red Top readers - and indeed their children - couldn't get enough of it.

And all that from one woman watching a child in front of the TV…

Spotting an idea is not easy. Although journalists are very good at spotting stories, we are notoriously *bad* at spotting new trends. It's only when the new trend has already been seized upon by another paper or a magazine that we belatedly realise that, for months now, this trend has been staring us in the face.

These little nuggets of journalistic gold are swirling all over the place, particularly on the internet and on TV and the radio.

The best way to describe it is that, say, you hear something on the radio and you think, "That's funny" or "That's odd" or, better still, "That's outrageous". That is the moment that you have to laser in to what, precisely, is so funny or so outrageous.

The punters on the street will have a giggle, or feel a moment's outrage, and then move on.

But a good hack sits up, pays attention and realises that if *they* find something amusing, or outrageous, then in all probability their readers will too.

This is newspaper gold. This is the sort of stuff that editors kill for - if, that is, they're trying to encourage creativity within the newsroom. And if you're an ideas-woman, you'll be far, far more versatile than a mere hard news hack who brings in his trusty exclusives. You'll be the sort of journalist that other papers want to poach and that, as we well know, is the only way to get a pay rise.

THE CHARMER…

Many commentators are predicting that by 2030, newspapers are going to be dead in the water. Instead we'll all be getting our news off the internet, the radio and possibly even the personalised chips that have been surgically implanted into our frontal lobes.

Personally, I reckon newspapers will always be around, if only to cater for that clique of die-hards like myself who just love the smell of newsprint in the morning.

The good news though for us humble news-gatherers is that it matters not one jot how our news stories are disseminated. Doesn't make any difference whether every word we write goes out on the net, or whether it is carved into tablets of polished Carrera marble. Because until Armageddon itself, there will always be a need for news stories. And although there will be faster and fancier ways of spreading these stories from one person to the next, as to the actual methods by which they are collected... well, I am cockily going to put my head on the block and predict that, even a millennium down the line, these techniques *still* won't have changed much. I don't doubt that when the Last Trump is finally called, there will be Red Top reporters out on Trafalgar Square asking punters just *"how they fee-e-e-el"* about the prospect of the world being swallowed into a Black Hole.

Because ultimately, news all boils down to the same thing: a hack getting alongside a punter who has witnessed something extraordinary and who is basking in their 15 minutes of fame.

Doesn't matter what newspaper, or what news outlet you're working on, this is one of the most basic skills of our trade. A good hack can crack open even the tough nuts who are standing there on the doorsteps with their arms folded and a sour "no comment" on their lips.

It takes great skill and considerable practice in order to become a good interviewer, and yet even though it is one of the essentials of our trade, I still find it staggering at how most novice hacks are just thrown in at the deep end. They're called over by the news editor, asked to interview the local minister, and sometimes they bodge it, and sometimes they don't, but either way they don't have the faintest idea of what they're about. It's all rather hit and miss. The problem is that most reporters have not been properly and specifically trained for the task in hand.

So let me explain. The key to an interview can be summed up in one very simple word: Charm.

Most people, when they imagine a Red Top reporter, conjure up this idea of a drooling Rottweiler, perhaps swearing at you with his black-capped foot stuck in the door. Well, I'm not saying that there aren't Red Top reporters like that... but the most successful reporters are invariably charmers.

We don't have to threaten people to get them to open up, we charm them. It's that bloody simple!

The main thing that reporters get wrong on a doorstep is that they forget to charm the interviewees. They're sent off, say, to Norfolk to interview some farmer whose daughter has just become the first woman in the world to swim across the Atlantic.

The mugs who go in on this sort of doorstep will immediately start hammering away with questions. "How did you feel... ", "What did you think... " - all that sort of stuff.

What they are forgetting is that before you do anything else in an interview, you HAVE to get a connection with the interviewee. Doesn't matter how you get the connection. But before you start pounding away with all your questions about the Atlantic swim, you have to be fully, fully connected with the interviewee.

This, invariably, is done by that ethereal, unquantifiable essence that is charm.

In Britain, the general rules of engagement say that you have to identify yourself and your paper before you crack on with the interviewee. Even this brief introduction is a chance for you to start applying your charm skills. Adopting a deferential tone, you identify who you're speaking to and then say, "I'm so sorry to bother you, it's Bill Coles from *The Sun*, I just wondered if I could have a very brief word about your daughter's swim across the Atlantic".

Who knows what's going to happen next? Maybe they'll let you in, maybe they've already been bought up and you'll get the door slammed in your face.

But whatever happens, you're going to start being charming, which means that you are going to change the subject to something that the interviewee would just love to talk about. This could be the garden; the roses in the garden; the dog in the garden; the kids' equipment in the garden; the weather; the pictures in the corridor as you walk through to the lounge; the set of golf clubs standing by the front door; the squalling toddler that is roaming round the kitchen.

It does not matter *how* you get the connection, but before you plunge into your gritty interview you *have* to have first forged a connection. And this, generally, is going to be done by talking about something that the interviewee enjoys talking about. Dogs, children, pastimes and gardens are generally a pretty safe bet. If the worst comes to the worst, you can talk about the weather, or the sporting event that's happening at the weekend. I don't care what you're going to be talking about. But what I do insist on is that you have properly connected with an interviewee before you start barking out questions. (There are, of course, exceptions, such as when the rest of the pack is endeavouring to spoil your exclusive. But even then, I'd still put my money on the charmer any day of the week.)

Only when the interviewee is fully on side, fully warmed up, and has offered you a nice cup of tea, is it okay to get out your notepad. (Though doubtless if you're a weasel you will already have your tape recorder whirring away in your top pocket.)

Getting the picture? On a doorstep, we only start the interview proper after the interviewee has been sufficiently charmed. Got it? Charmed.

And here's something that a lot of veteran hacks still haven't appreciated. Gatekeepers need charming too.

If you're trying to get at a bereaved mum, then very often you'll have to get past some doughty relative who's acting as a gatekeeper. Well guess what happens if you don't charm the gatekeeper? You'll just get the door slammed in your face.

So when the gatekeeper is fending you off, you should be exerting your considerable charm skills on them too. If you've really got them on side, they can even act as a sort of ambassador, actually presenting you to the main star of the show.

And if you don't apply charm...

Ah yes. Well I know of many, many stories that have gone awry because the reporters have failed to apply charm; been involved in a number of them too.

But perhaps the most spectacular example of charm - and the lack of it - came with the amber-coloured football that was used in the final of the 1966 World Cup. England beat Germany 4-2 after a hat-trick from Geoff Hurst and, according to tradition, Geoff should have gone home with the match-ball.

He didn't.

Some thirty years later, England was in the throes of another championship, the European Cup. From out of nowhere, someone raises an obscure question: what the hell happened to Geoff Hurst's hat-trick ball?

It turns out that at the end of the match, a German player, Helmut Haller, had picked up the ball from the back of the net and then taken it home. The ball had spent the next thirty years languishing in the cellar of his restaurant near Munich.

Britain's Red Top papers were all over the story.

The race was on to get the ball back to Britain. They all wanted it. And from a personal point of view, all I can say is that I thank my stars that I was not involved in *The Sun*'s mission. It was a total catastrophe.

The Sun sent a team of heavyweight reporters and photographers - six of them. Six! They arrived in early at Haller's restaurant and immediately opened the negotiations to buy the ball.

They didn't get very far. It's hard to pinpoint what, exactly, went wrong. But I've got a pretty shrewd idea...

The *Mirror*, meanwhile, sent along one roughy-tough photographer and one solitary reporter, Peter Allen. Now Peter has a merry tinkling laugh and a lovely winsome smile. He's very unthreatening and, as the mood takes him, is even capable of being a serious schmoozer.

Guess who got the ball?

The Sun hacks were trounced by a single *Mirror* reporter and then tried to hide their shame by claiming that Peter could speak German. Absolute piffle! Peter couldn't speak a word of German. But what he did have in spades was the one thing that the entire *Sun* team had failed to apply. Charm.

As it happens, Peter even got a book out of the whole tale: *An Amber Glow*. It's a fantastic story, and in the middle of the book you will see a picture of Peter standing between two veteran German footballers. Peter is looking clean-cut, presentable, and with a nice smile playing over his fresh-faced cheeks. Now that man, my friend, is the compleat Red Top charmer.

AND HOW TO BECOME

A CHARMER…

A lot of people believe that charm is something you're simply born with. You've either got it or you ain't, and if you haven't got it, then you're destined to spend the rest of your miserable life blundering through this swamp of social ineptitude.

Of course there are some natural-born charmers. I'd be pretty certain that Bill Clinton was twinkling from the first moment that he set foot on this earth.

But what I'm telling you now is that charm is a skill which can be learned and practised every single day.

The problem with trying to apply charm on a doorstep interview is that if you haven't had much practice, then you'll be nervous. This nerviness quickly transmits itself to the interviewee, who in turn will feel uncomfortable and want to bring the whole thing to a halt as quickly as possible.

So what I'm suggesting is that before you're sent off on these big, big doorsteps, you first learn to become a charmer in low-key, low-stress situations.

How about… just for the sake of argument… buying a newspaper. You go into a newsagent, get your newspaper and your stick of gum, and then, well, rather than just saying, "Thank you, bye-bye," you endeavour to see whether you can… wait for it now… forge a connection with the newsagent.

I know what you're already probably thinking, it's just so simple!

Well of course it is. But if it's so goddamn simple, then how come no-one, on any of these media courses all over the world, is suggesting this pitifully simple course of action?

All you'll be trying to do is see if you can connect with strangers. So in future, whenever you have a transaction with a shop assistant, getting the petrol, buying a pint, or even asking for directions - you're going to see if you can connect. Raise a smile. Make them actually want to talk to you.

At a novice level, you can just ask them, "How's your day going so far?" (slightly superior to "How's it going?"). But ultimately you're looking to be so fly on your feet that you're able to *banter* with these strangers. You throw the ball in the air, they hit it, and it doesn't matter where they hit it, you are now going to pick it up and hurl it straight back. But with just a little bit of topspin.

So if they want to talk about tennis, then that, surprisingly, will be the subject that you'll be diving into. If it's children or newspapers, then guess what words will be burbling from your lips.

You are going to be seeing if you can forge a connection with these strangers; make them smile; make them tell you about their lives. Checkout staff are a gold mine, because with them, you can be chatting for three or four minutes; ample enough time for a charmer.

Just consider what will have happened in four months' time. That'll be, say, 5 strangers a day for 120 days. That'll be 600 chances to practise your charm skills on a wide variety of different people.

If you've got any better way of learning how to be a charmer, I'd love to hear it.

The beauty of chatting up these strangers is that it's very low-key. You can experiment. Doesn't make any difference if you mess up because it's not remotely important.

But, come the day when you do have an important interview, you will be in a far, far better position to exhibit all your newly-won charm skills.

Some people say that practising your charm on strangers is "manipulative". I couldn't disagree more. We are trying to engage with them. And the funny thing is that when you engage with somebody - no matter how trivial the transaction - the whole business becomes much more enjoyable. Rather than continuing to live in your own little bubble, you have extended yourself; you have touched a stranger.

A lot of people can't be bothered to chat to sales-staff, and the main reason is because it takes *energy*. Rather than just being on your usual autopilot, your little brain is whirring, your antennae are flickering and all the while you are gauging when to strike with a quip. You are POURING energy into the conversation and sometimes it can seem like a whole lot of effort for scant reward. Even I find it pretty tough to get going before I've had my first coffee of the day.

However... If you do start connecting with strangers, you will find that unusual things begin to happen. Little perks. Upgrades at the airport. Discounts. All manner of weird things will start happening to you. Is it just happenstance? Or could it just happen to be because you have connected with a stranger who has it in their power to do you a favour...

And while I'm on the subject. Just a terribly minor thing. Not even *remotely* important. But I guarantee that within a few months, you'll be able to chat up strangers like a pro. That cocktail party. That conference. That gorgeous stranger who you've been eyeing up for the past two hours. You see it's not about chat-up lines. It's about banter. A little light stroke that's been applied with finesse.

Who would have dreamed that a book about Red Top hackery could have so quickly segued into a seduction manual?

One last thing: it's not everyone's cup of tea, but cold-selling is the perfect way to learn how to charm a stranger. When my first novel came out, I was sent off for a signing session to the local bookshop. I very quickly realised that if I spent the day sitting behind my desk, I'd sell just two books.

So instead, I treated my signing session as an exercise in cold-selling. This is a very difficult thing to do. Unlike the shop assistants, you are trying to forge a connection with a stranger who has precisely zero interest in you or what you have to offer. It takes balls.

Some people are rude; some are utterly delightful. But boy is it the most brilliant way of learning the arcane gift of charm, and how to apply it.

MANNERS

Real charmers have impeccable manners.

Workaday hacks might imagine that manners are irrelevant when it comes to an interview. They could not be more wrong.

When we meet a stranger, we make up our minds very, very quickly. And believe you me, all these infinitesimal details such as your dress, your speech and your manners are all being weighed up before somebody allows you into their house.

So, what this means in practice is that we like to leave things as we find them. If the garden gate is closed when we arrive at a house, then we shut it after we've walked through. If there's a chain across the drive, then that will also be replaced.

If you're a guy, then good manners means that now, tomorrow, and for all time, you will hold the door open for every single person you meet, IRRESPECTIVE OF THEIR SEX. On occasion, this may mean that you're left holding the door for twenty charmless tourists, not one of whom has the courtesy to say thank you. Doesn't matter. Doesn't matter one jot. Always, always, hold the door open. This is not just good manners. It is also a subtle power play. When you hold the door open, it shows, in a very, very delicate way that you are the boss. Just watch Barack Obama welcoming dignitaries into the White House. He will always follow them in afterwards. Without exception.

When it comes to drinks, or meals, do not be shy about coming forward. Make it a point of being FIRST IN to buy the drinks, rather than the tightwad in the corner who never reaches for his wallet. Generosity counts. We like it. We like it a lot.

When those drinks have been bought and you're saying "Cheers" or "Here's to us", look your fellow drinkers in the eye. In South Africa, not looking your drinking-mates in the eye is considered such bad form that you'll be cursed with "seven years of bad sex".

At a meal - well it goes without saying that you're not a chomper. You're not spraying food all over the place. Further to that, Uncle Billy's Rule states that YOU CANNOT HELP YOURSELF TO ANYTHING AT ALL WITHOUT FIRST OFFERING IT TO YOUR DINING COMPANIONS. If you're about to top up your glass, then first you have to top up the glasses of everyone else around you. If you want more potatoes, then you have to offer them around first.

While I'm on the subject. We don't start a meal before the host or hostess has started. Doubtless they'll already have said, "Do start without me!" FORGET IT! Only mugs take them at their word. Much more stylish to start when your host eventually dives in. Who the hell cares if your food has already gone stone cold?

Similarly, it is not good form to start slurping your drink down before everyone is set. You will feel one hell of a prat if the guy whose bought the drinks finally arrives at the table and you've already downed half a pint.

Call me old-fashioned, but I also like to see the guys stand up when - in a social situation - a woman enters the room.

One more thing. Mobile phones. If ever you're in company, whether it's a drink or a dinner, then can you kindly turn off your bloody phone? Or at least put it on vibrate.

I was chatting to a self-styled charmer a few days ago, and admittedly we were waiting for the kids to come out of some after-school class, but he's spending half his time diddling around on his phone looking through his wretched messages. And then even as I'm talking to him – something of huge import, obviously – there he is actually RESPONDING to an email.

This is wrong on so many levels. When you are with a person, even if you have just happened to have met them on the street, then you give them FULL FOCUS! You do not constantly check your phone for emails – and if it is one of the mad-masters who's calling you up, then take the call, and smile sweetly, and ask if it would be alright to call them back.

Nobody is ever going to feel warmly towards you if your little phone and its messages are more important than the here and the now of the conversation that you're having.

That probably covers the most important bases for a hack. There are loads more. I remember getting bollocked by some grande dame for reading the papers at the breakfast table. Slightly debatable that one. But anyway, the point is that we charmers are polite, well-mannered. Studiously courteous.

THE EYES

Gentlemen hacks - I have news for you.

As I'm sure you know, it's a good idea to look people in the eyes.

But when you're dealing with a woman, you should be holding her gaze for much longer. MUCH longer. As long as you possibly can. Doesn't matter if somebody drops a cup, if there's an explosion going off in the next building, keep your eyes GLUED to the woman's. Do not let them go.

I guess what I'm basically saying is that it is impossible to hold a woman's gaze for too long.

Men on the other hand, well they don't like it if you hold their gaze too long. Makes them think you're kinky, or you fancy them. It freaks them out a little.

But women - I promise you - want you to hold their gaze.

Although I've been a hack for twenty-three years, I only appreciated this subtle point about ten years ago. The effects can be amazing. Just try it! Try it!

It's said that the greatest charmer on earth, Bill Clinton, would give women the "big ears". He'd sit down, listen to them, and for a few minutes they believed they were the most important woman in the world to this man; didn't matter what else was going on, Bill had full lock-on.

But on a slight point of detail, I don't think Clinton was using his ears; he was using his eyes. When he's talking to a woman, his eyes don't even flicker for a moment.

So, seeing as eye contact is so absolutely essential, it goes without saying that all sunglasses have to come off. How can you charm someone if they're just staring into a pair of mirror-shades? (I know this is a statement of the bleeding obvious, but you'd be staggered at the number of really senior hacks who still conduct interviews with shades on.)

There are other little details about charm and, of course, seduction, as the two go hand in hand.

When appropriate, a little touch can work well. But not the shoulder or the back. Usually a touch to the elbow works best - friendly, but still formal.

First names. As any idiot knows, first names are very, very important. Using someone's first name is like giving them a very light stroke. Once you've got someone's first name, then lightly sprinkle it into the conversation. Salesmen, who also style themselves as charmers, like to use your first name every other sentence. But we hacks are genuine charmers. So although we're aware of the power of first names, we don't use them too often.

But be careful about first names. Middle-aged people can get very crusty if they're addressed by their first name, so tread carefully with them. Keep things formal until they've given you permission to use their first name.

As for you, well of course you want people to call you by your first name. It's softer. The usual drill, when people ask my name, is to say, "It's Bill, Bill Coles. But do call me Bill."

So much friendlier than saying, "The name's Bond. James Bond."

Thank Yous. We like Thank Yous - a lot. If you've seen anyone for any sort of drink or meal, then text or email a brief note of thanks. If it's been a lavish meal, then it's time for a handwritten note.

Thank yous may take barely a minute to do. But they aren't just about good manners. They're about giving your contact a light stroke of the elbow; that's good.

Only one in ten people ever bother to send a thank you note. So if you get into the habit, then you will stand head and shoulders above the rest of the herd.

I noticed this recently with a team of reporters that I'd been working with. At the end of the course, we had some group photos taken. A week later, I emailed the best pix round to all the reporters.

It was very telling who sent a thank you email. Only a few dropped me a line. But the hacks who did reply were, without exception, the hot ones. The ones who were really going places.

One last little thing while we're on the subject of charm. Very often while you're trying to forge a connection with an interviewee, you'll see that they've got their arms crossed. This, as I'm sure you know, is not good news. It means they're not all receptive to any of the words and ideas that you're spouting. They're not nearly warmed up enough for you to start interviewing them.

If you see this, it can work quite well to physically break down the barrier. You offer them a piece of paper, or a newspaper, and, by accepting the piece of paper, they uncross their arms. It seems surprising, but they will now start listening to your patter.

DANGER - EMAILS!

Would it be at all possible for you to do yourself a LARGE favour and start treating emails as if they're as lethal as a stick of gelignite. They are so bloody dangerous. And the thing about emails is that they never, ever go away.

I'll bet you've been told this before. It is so obvious! Don't commit anything that is even remotely dodgy to an email. Can I possibly make it any simpler?

Alright, I'll try. In future, for every email that you write at work and probably at home, you want to imagine that you're copying in not just the editor, but the Director of Public Prosecutions. Got it?

Well you've probably got it, but I can tell you that there are still scores of hacks out there who are sending on sordid jokes to their mates. And what happens if you bring the name of your paper into disrepute? Well it's bye-bye. Red Top papers have got to be absolutely squeaky clean. They're dishing it out to the adulterous celebs and the fraudulent agents and they can't afford to have their name sullied by a reporter whose been sending out filthy emails. So if there's a commotion over some smutty email that's been sent from your paper, then the reporter's got to go, otherwise the paper will stand accused of rank hypocrisy.

Why should you imagine that all your emails are being copied over to the Director of Public Prosecutions? Because, my friend, when the shit hits the fan - as it surely will - he is going to be the guy that's reading your emails!

For the last five years, *The Sun*'s sister paper, the now defunct *News of the World* has been embroiled in a phone-hacking scandal. The paper's Royal Editor, Clive Goodman, had been employing a private detective to hack into the mobile phone messages of the stars.

Initially, it was just Clive and his lackey who went to jail, but two years later, the phone-hacking scandal exploded back onto the front pages when *The Guardian* revealed that some 3,000 stars had had their mobiles hacked.

Cue a massive police investigation. Cue the *News of the World* having to hand over ALL of their emails. Cue the end of the paper and a load of the mad-masters facing the distinct possibility of jail.

Ahem! May I just ask one question? What on earth is going on here? How on earth did these senior execs allow themselves to be trapped by something as mundane as an email?

The email trail never goes away. Even years later, it can come back to haunt you.

So, I'm certainly not recommending that you do anything dodgy. These days I like to keep everything above board. But if you *are* doing something that's, perhaps, just a little underhand, then can you kindly not leave any tracks? Get a disposable pay as you go mobile. (Yes, believe it or not, the Director of Public Prosecutions is quite capable of going through all your phone records.)

And, whatever you do, keep those work emails CLEAN.

I currently know of four journalists who are hording up various ranting emails from their mad-masters. Why are they storing them up? For that golden day when they feel that it's time to jump ship and they can claim "constructive dismissal". Know how much a Red Top sports sub got recently for being bullied out of his job by one of the mad-masters? I think he had an out-of-court settlement of around £750,000. Nice work, eh?

One last little gem - from my days on *The Sun*.

There was an absolutely gorgeous member of staff who, to save her blushes, we shall call Imogen.

Imogen was having an affair with the editor of a rival paper. This was the editor of the *Mirror*, and since this man is completely without shame, I have no problem whatsoever in naming him: Piers Morgan.

Piers was married with kids. Imogen, I think, was just recently married.

But, you know how it happens, the pair had met up, and the chemistry had been like a couple of electricity pylons clashing together during a freak storm.

Leaky place though, Fleet Street, a bit gossipy.

Particularly when a Red Top editor happens to be having a fling with a staff reporter from his direct rival.

I may be wrong about this, but I think that when the *Sun* executives got to hear about the whole thing and started trawling through Imogen's inbox, they found over 2,000 of Piers' emails.

She was out within the hour. (And went on to have a very successful career on one of the broadsheets, so - who the hell knows? - maybe it was all for the best.)

AND FINDING MORE

EXCLUSIVES

Although most Red Top hacks are pretty good at spotting news stories they're notoriously bad at spotting the softer stories that pop up right in front of their noses. Literally. These are the light, frothy stories that are cropping up every day via emails and Facebook.

Now these little jokey stories may not have the same weight as a hard-hitting crime story, but they can still make page leads. They're still making spreads. They are making the readers laugh, or shake their heads and, along with the gore, the showbiz, the telly and the sport, they are an essential part of the tabloid mix.

I once did up a quirky little story on a mechanic who'd turned his sofa into a car. Great pictures of him driving along the road. I'd thought it might be a page lead. But there was so little news that day that it ended up as *The Sun*'s splash.

So next time you see anything remotely weird, amusing or fantastical on Facebook or YouTube, then those alarm bells should be jangling, telling you that if *you* are finding it funny, then almost certainly your readers will find it funny too.

Finding a peg for your funny photo is going to be the very least of your problems. Usually the stories nose on the "quirky film that's taking the internet by storm… " Then, in time-honoured fashion, you merely lift all the pictures, take the best quotes, and you've got yourself a spread.

Recently on Facebook, I saw a funny picture that was entitled, "The House That Looks Like Hitler". Unfortunately I was out of the country at the time, otherwise I'd have flogged it myself to the British Red Tops, whose readers still adore stories about Hitler and the Nazis.

What amazed me though, was that it was another THREE DAYS before the photo finally ran in the British tabloids. And yet The Hitler House picture must have been seen by scores of hacks before somebody finally made the connection and realised that it might be a good news story.

So if anybody's sending you a funny YouTube link that's new and fresh, you should immediately be working out how to get it into the paper.

Similarly, when you are laughing at an embarrassing round-robin email that's just gone viral, you should be weighing up its news values. Every month or so in the Red Tops there's another story about some young swain whose passionate and private email has suddenly been blasted into the internet stratosphere. In future, when you receive these emails, start thinking "Story!".

YouTube is getting loads of cracking videos every day. Have a little trawl through in the morning to see if there's anything fresh.

In Britain, most stars' Twitter feeds and blogs are being closely monitored by the Red Tops. But outside the UK, the Red Tops are not nearly so vigilant. Sign up to your stars' blogs and Twitter feeds - particularly the B-listers' blogs - and watch the exclusives roll in.

While I'm at it: in the UK at the moment, there are a large number of global stars who have issued "Super-Injunctions" which are preventing the British Red Tops from publishing the details of their sordid extramarital sex lives.

These super-injunctions only carry weight in the UK. But most of the stars' names are all out there on Twitter and Google. So why aren't the foreign Red Tops getting stuck in and naming and shaming all these litigious A-listers? Just a thought.

HUMOUR...

Doesn't matter where you are in the world, whether it's America, Britain, Africa or the Far East, it's going to be a pretty safe bet that the core Red Top readers are going to have a sense of humour.

Damned if I know specifically what they're going to find funny. In Germany, for instance, there exists a comic who has near God-like status. His name is Freddie Frinton, a British comedian who died some years ago and who has been all but forgotten in the UK. But in Germany, and across large swathes of Eastern Europe, Frinton has achieved a quite mythical status.

It's all down to a 15 minute sketch, Dinner For One, in which Frinton plays the role of a butler during a bizarre birthday party. The table is set for five people, but there's only one person there - the hostess, Miss Sophie. As for the four empty seats, these are seemingly taken up by Miss Sophie's past loves. Throughout the dinner, Frinton keeps topping up the "guests'" glasses, and ends up getting paralytically drunk as he polishes off all the drinks himself.

Frinton also has a catchline, which he repeats over and over again to Miss Sophie - "The same procedure as last year?" Now I'll guarantee you one thing, if you are in Germany and you're endeavouring to practise your charm-skills on a stranger, then all you have to say is, "The same procedure as last year?" and they will instantly - instantly! - give you the most beaming smile. Strange, but that's the sort of cult following Frinton has in Germany.

Anyway - Dinner For One is now such a big part of the New Year's Eve routine in Germany that, year in, year out, over half the country are watching it. They have Dinner For One parties, and a lot of Germans can quote the sketch absolutely word for word.

I was intrigued enough to have a look at the sketch on YouTube. It was slightly amusing, I can't really say better than that. But my son, Dexter, found it absolutely side-splitting.

So I admit that I don't know what, specifically, is going to tickle the Red Top readers' funny bone, but I do know they love to have a laugh. And I do know that humour is an essential part of the mix that goes to make up mass-market entertainment.

And I believe there's not nearly enough humour in the Red Tops.

Most tabloids will have some sort of strip cartoon as well as a joke or two, some funny letters, and possibly a sketch by the paper's resident cartoonist which will invariably be devoid of any humour whatsoever.

There are also, occasionally, cute pictures of animals or kids doing funny things.

I would like to see humour becoming a mainstream part of the paper, one of the pivots. You open up the paper and you know that somewhere in there you'll find something that is going to give you a damn good laugh.

There are a number of ways this can be done and, I am fully aware that this is going to vary from country to country.

But one of the most obvious ways is to have a riff on the previous day's news. Day One it's announced that a kangaroo is on the loose just outside London; Day Two, they're playing it for laughs, and a reporter dresses up in full Safari gear to see if he can spot the rogue Roo.

Or, in South Africa, on Day One it's revealed that they have discovered the country's biggest pothole, an absolute monster that can swallow a whole car; Day Two, and we're playing it for laughs and you might turn the pothole into a pool for a Page Three girl; Day Three, you could fill the hole up with an entire family, it's bigger than a house!

Humour is a light, easy way of taking a story a step further. It's not a new line. It's a new take on a situation, maximising its comic potential; if you hit a rich seam, the gag can last for months.

But, as ever, you don't want to do too many of these whacky riffs on a story. Everything, please, in moderation. Unless, of course, the readers are gobbling it up.

AND RITUAL HUMILIATION...

On *The Sun*, they had a very peculiar way of blooding their reporters - just to see whether they were tough enough, spunky enough, to take whatever was thrown at them.

I've come across a number of Red Top reporters who believe that they are pure news-hounds, and who think that it's frankly beneath them to sully their hands on jokey features. (Don't they get bored out of their minds?)

But to me, a decent Red Top hack can turn their hand to anything: tear-jerking news features, hard-hitting news exclusives, and yes, on occasion, even taking one for the team.

What I'm talking about is a particular type of news story that I guess can be roughly summed up under the term: "Humiliate the reporter". And when I use the word "humiliate", I do not use it lightly. It can be quite fantastically embarrassing…

So perhaps I should tell you how *The Sun*'s executives used to blood their rising stars. I have one particular young star's story to tell. It's a great one.

It was my own.

You wouldn't remember the movie, but about eighteen years ago, there was a film out called *To Wong Foo, Thanks for Everything, Julie Newmarr*. It starred Patrick Swayze who played the role of a cross-dresser driving through the desert. And in those days, the executives only had to hear the words "cross-dresser movie" and, like Pavlov's Dog, they'd start salivating.

So, on the day of the *To Wong Foo* premiere, I was dispatched hither and thither all about London wearing an exact copy of Patrick Swayze's outfit, namely: silver boots with six inch heels; a skin-tight purple sequined dress that barely covered by thighs; and all topped off by a foot-high beehive of red hair. In all, I was at least 7'6" tall. Quite an imposing sight.

Off I paraded around London town. I remember posing for pictures outside Bank station as a city slicker walked past. "That must have been one big, big bet you lost," he said.

Later, I tried to take Natasha, my high-flying girlfriend, out for a five-star lunch having carefully neglected to tell her about by new look. She came out of the revolving doors. Took one look at me. And went straight back in again.

All good knockabout stuff for the sizzling copy that I'd be writing later.

At the premiere, I buttonholed Swayze himself, grabbing him by the shoulder as I grinned at my cameraman.

"What do you think about my outfit?" I said.

He looked me up and down, rather askance. "You've worked hard at it," he said.

Terrific!

I didn't know it at the time, but I was in very exalted company. My editor Stuart Higgins had had to do the exact same thing when Dustin Hoffman's starred as the cross-dressing *Tootsie*. (Just *en passant*. Now I don't know how this can possibly have occurred, because usually the News International library is about the most efficient newspaper library on earth, but when Stuart became the boss, somewhere along the way those Tootsie pictures just disappeared… Where *ever* could they have got to?)

Mind you, it could have been *much* worse. A few years ago in Britain, there stormed onto the front pages a mildly eccentric guy who was known as The

Naked Rambler. He was trying to walk the length of Britain in the nude. He seemed to spend most of his time locked up in jail. (And, well over a decade later, he's still being locked up.)

A good friend, Tom Newton Dunn, then a staff reporter on the *Mirror*, was despatched off to interview the Naked Rambler - in the nude. Talk about taking one for the team! The pictures of Tom and the Naked Rambler strutting about in the buff were absolutely jaw-dropping. (Obviously Tom's crown jewels were pixelated for the newspaper article - but the original pix went round the entire newsroom in approximately five seconds flat. And there I should perhaps draw a discreet veil over the matter, though I think I can possibly mention that Tom's stock skyrocketed among certain female members of the *Mirror* staff - and, further to that, Tom currently resides as the Political Editor of *The Sun*. Taking one for the team shows, rather surprisingly, that you're a team player.)

AND SATIRE

Satire can be a hilarious tool for sending up politicians, sportsmen and budding starlets. But it's a very dangerous weapon. Politicians, in particular, tend to take themselves very seriously, and the one thing they just can't bear is being publicly mocked.

Britain has a long history of satire and for centuries now, politicians have known that having the piss taken out of them was all part of the rub of public life.

So on the day of the 1997 General Election, *The Sun* turned the Tory Party leader William Hague into a dead parrot. Fifteen years earlier, The Labour leader Neil Kinnock was morphed into a light bulb, along with the legendary front page, "If Neil Kinnock wins the election, will the last person to leave Britain turn the lights out."

It's now routine at election time for British politicians to be followed by squads of hacks dressed up as chickens or blue-blood toffs.

But in other countries, where the politicians are not quite so robust, they can go completely mad if they think they've been turned into a public joke.

That's not to say that a Red Top shouldn't satirise politicians. Satire is a fantastic way of sexing up the humdrum world of politics for a Red Top reader. But it just means that in countries where the whole subject of politics is a little sensitive, then you've got to be particularly light on your toes.

In South Africa recently, the general election was ten days away, and we were exploring ways to satirise the leading politicians.

"What about President Zuma and all his wives?" I asked. "Is that worth having a pop at?"

The executives grimaced. In general, it's never worth having a pop at President Zuma. It's bound to annoy him and it will probably annoy half the country.

The conversation moved on to Zuma's dancing. Zuma is a very good dancer, and a great singer also. When he's performing on the stump, he's stupendous.

One of the South African executives happened to mention that Zuma's leading rival, Helen Zille, had been having dancing and singing lessons so that she also could put on a turn for the electorate.

Bingo!

The spread headline was, "Political Idol - The Dance-Off".

One of the executives then milked the gag by buttonholing Zuma at a press briefing (See PRESS CONFERENCES). "What do you think of Helen Zille's dancing technique?" he asked. "Have you got any tips for her?"

Satirising sports stars is a lot easier than sending up the politicians. It is true that the sports stars are likely to be just as self-important as the politicians, but they don't have the power.

In Britain, sportsmen are routinely mocked on the back pages for their stupid haircuts, their complicated love lives or their fat bellies.

One style of satire that can be very effective is sending up the national team when it's lost. Normally when the national team loses at a particular sport, then the story runs for a day before it's dropped. Let's forget about it. It's over. Nobody wants to talk about it.

But if you start sending up the coach - or the team itself - then the gag can run for weeks. A few years back in a European Cup, the England football team were playing like donkeys, so I spent a fortnight trekking back and forth across England with a donkey in the back of a horse-truck. The donkey and I would then watch the next match in a pub, with the boozed-up fans telling me exactly what they thought of the England team's performance.

Another example from another dud, was when England were beaten 2-1 by Sweden. The sports subs dreamt up a truly memorable headline: "Swedes 2, Turnips 1" - and then milked the vegetable gag right up until the day when Graham Taylor was sacked as manager, when his head was morphed onto a turnip under the headline, "That's Yer Allotment".

THE SILVER TONGUE...

Sometimes in the newsroom, you will hear a reporter or an executive who can charm the very birds from the trees. This is a woman, or a man, who has developed an astonishing ability to work a telephone. They have the Silver Tongue.

If you're going to learn one single thing from this book, then here it is: sit yourself down next to that silver-tongued charmer. Every opportunity you get, plant yourself next to the Silver Tongue's desk, and let those words wash over you. Devour every morsel. And, perhaps, after a few months, you may find that you have become a Silver Tongue.

Naturally, there are other ways of learning the Silver Tongue, but this is Route One to becoming a charmer on the phone.

I learned it next to the desk of the legendary Fleet Street reporter John Kay - journalist of the year, scoop of the year; his awards are legion. After about six months of having me sit next to him, John turned to me and said to me, "Do you know Bill, I was listening to you just then, and I was wondering where on earth I'd heard those words before, and then it came to me! It's like listening to a recording of myself, though slightly more la-di-da. No offence, mind." None taken, John.

Ideally, we like to be face to face with an interviewee so that we can look them in the eye and start exerting our considerable charm skills. Very often, however, they're halfway round the world, which means we will instead have to apply the Silver Tongue.

As ever, it takes a lot of practice. Did you think this business of becoming a Red Top hack was going to be easy? It only took me about ten years before I thought I could cut it - and even then, I still wasn't even close.

The principles of the Silver Tongue are much the same as those for a doorstep. We only start hammering away with our hard-hitting questions once we're fully connected with the interviewee. They've got to be warmed up. On side. Smiling.

Smiles - and indeed boredom - can be heard over the phone. Smile a lot, joke, laugh. The skill of the Silver Tongue is that you are trying to get some connection outside the subject in hand. From the CEO to the drudge press officer at the police station, they all want to be treated as humans; they want a little bit of jokey banter. Unless, of course, if it's inappropriate, like a bereavement.

Even if it's just a quip and a brief laugh, you have to have forged some connection before you get onto the workaday subject of your story.

So, just like on a doorstep, we're going to start off in our softest, gentlest voice, and your opening line should be so well-grooved that you can recite it in your sleep. It goes something like this:

Punter: "Hello?"

Hack: "Oh hello, Mr Smith?" (First of all you're ascertaining if you're speaking to the right person.)

Punter: "Yes, who's that?"

Here's your opening line, spoken very softly: "Oh I'm VERY SORRY TO BOTHER YOU Mr Smith, it's Bill Coles here from *The Sun* newspaper."

"Yes?"

"I WAS JUST WONDERING IF I COULD HAVE A BRIEF WORD ABOUT…"

What these opening sentences have done is 1. Found out that you're talking to the right person. 2. Put you in a position of deference. And 3. You've declared who you are.

In the UK, you've got to declare yourself. It's part of the rules of engagement. Things are more easygoing in other countries, so it's not necessary to immediately say that you're a hack or which paper you're from. But do remember that if you initially hide the fact that you're a hack, then many punters will just slam the phone down when they eventually learn where you're from. (Though it can work well. Occasionally punters will be so charmed that they're only too happy to talk.)

You're now looking to get that connection. You could try repeating again, "I'm sorry to bother you at a time like this, when I'm sure you'd much rather be outside enjoying the amazing weather… " or you could try: "Watching the amazing cricket/rugby/golf on the TV… "

What you're probing for in the first minute is anything you can latch onto which will show that you're not just a robo-hack, you're a warm empathetic human being. So while they're yacking away, your antennae have to be fully attuned to what's coming over, and if they happen to mention their car, or their garden, or their holiday, then you pick up on that. And flick it back to them. Give it a little bit of spin.

The general rule for phones is the same for doorsteps. Most punters are polite and civilised. And if they've got a nice person on the phone, they'll be nice back. They may not be chatty, they may not want to talk. But… they won't slam the phone down. What this means is that on a tricky call, you are going to keep on talking and talking until you're blue in the face. You won't stop until they've physically cut you off.

First names, as ever, are great. If they ask who you are, give your full name, and say, "But do call me Bill/Claire, etc." If at all appropriate, use their first name. Like on doorsteps, watch out for people in their fifties and over, who may want to stick to surnames.

You should aim to drop their name into the conversation about three or four times; some morons drop it in every sentence, but that is way too much. It's meant to be subtle and permeating their subconscious. Using first names every sentence is like using a sledgehammer; it's what sales-people are trained to do, and a reporter's charm skills are FAR, FAR superior to those of a jobbing salesman.

Just like on the doorsteps, it's important to remember that GATEKEEPERS NEED CHARMING TOO.

If you piss off the secretary, or the receptionist, they won't even put you through. So banter a bit with the gatekeepers. If you can get a laugh, that is good. It should be standard procedure from now on that you are charming to every person you speak to on the phone. It's good practice and it makes for better service. Be especially charming to spouses. It doesn't matter if you're looking to get hold of a Chief Executive at home for an urgent story, if the spouse answers the phone, then lay it on thick. Do not sell yourself short. It's a big, big error to just brusquely ask for the Chief Executive and be quick about it. If you get hold of the spouse, joke about all the late hours the boss has been doing, or the amount of press coverage they've been having. It does not matter what you banter about, but DO NOT FORGET THE BANTER. No-one likes to be treated as a bloody minion - least of all a spouse. (Treat a spouse badly and you can be quite certain that not two minutes after the call, they will be saying, "Who was that vile person... ")

Just on a matter of office politics, the person that you have to lay it on thickest with is the boss' partner. You know why? Because the boss' partner is, believe it or not, the person they're going to end up in bed with. Chatting to them on the phone? Charm. Chatting to them at the office party? Charm. Look them in the eyes. Be interested. Never, ever abandon them - they feel like enough of a fish out of water, without being dumped by some poxy reporter.

All tricky phone calls have to be recorded. This should now be mandatory. If you think it might get nasty - if there's even the remotest chance of the lawyers being called in - then record that call. If it's not recorded and it should have been, then the reporter can expect to be kicked - heartily - round the newsroom.

At the end of your call, you are going to check the person's name, their age, their address, their job, (and if appropriate the number of children and if they're married.) You're also going to ask for their home, work and mobile numbers. The numbers are most important, because later in the day you will doubtless be asked to ask more questions - and if you can't get hold of your own interviewee, then the news editor will soon have steam coming out of his ears.

One more general tip: If it's a difficult call, stand up. Makes you feel more dynamic, it energises your voice. But above all, remember that if you want to become a Silver Tongue, then sit yourself next to a Silver Tongue.

AND HOW TO LEARN IT

I realise that it's all too possible that you *don't* have a Silver Tongue in the office, so there's no-one to sit yourself beside to learn it all first-hand.

Doesn't matter. Doesn't matter one jot.

You're just going to have to learn the Silver Tongue by yourself. And, like learning to interview people, this is done by chatting up strangers on the phone.

Whenever you're talking to a stranger on the phone, whether it's a receptionist, a copytaker, a secretary or a booking clerk, you are going to start exerting your immense charm-skills to see if you can forge a connection and MAKE THEM LAUGH.

That is your challenge. Might be just a little impish quip about the latest events in politics or sport, it does not matter. It is going to be whatever line crops up in that fertile brain of yours that will, preferably, be original and will show the person at the other end of the line that you're putting in a little bit of graft especially for them.

The more you do it, the better you'll get. And, just as with charming the newsagents and the florists, you will soon find that you're getting much more out of these conversations. Of course you're just larking around, having some fun - and what, in heaven, is so wrong with that? - but it is also one of the very best ways of practising the Silver Tongue.

And if you don't practice the Silver Tongue, what will happen? Well it's very simple. You will continue to have short, curt conversations on the phone; you will continue to get phones slammed down on you; and the news editor will very quickly realise that when it comes to delivering the goods from a phoner, frankly you're not up to it.

Just one more thing about practising the Silver Tongue. And I know that, yet again, I'm stating the bleeding obvious. (And yet you would not believe the number of veteran hacks who still haven't got it.) But let's suppose you've got some big, big interview coming up. Let's say it's some British woman who's been jailed for murder in America; she's facing life behind bars; and after one hell of a lot of work, you've actually got her on the phone. Your tape-recorder is whirring away. The interviewee is very nervous, and then you're off! You're on your own. It's now all down to you and your Silver Tongue. (You have already guessed, I hope, that this scenario did actually happen to me.)

Well would you rather be still trying to hone your Silver Tongue skills during this important interview - or would you rather have improved your technique over the previous year during countless little phone conversations with strangers?

Some people are born with charm and the Silver Tongue. But for the rest of the Great Unwashed, it only comes through months and months of practice. You can be trained up to your eyeballs, but there can never be any substitute for actually practising your charm-skills on strangers.

THE SILVER TONGUE - AND ITS FLAWS

There is a big problem with the Silver Tongue, and the better you get at it, the bigger the problem.

The problem is that it is so damn easy connecting with people over the phone, that you forget it is still essential to meet people face to face.

The Silver Tongue is the perfect tool for quickly extracting information via the phone. If it's a one-off interview with someone who happens to be revelling in their 15 minutes of fame, then it'll be just dandy.

But do not ever, ever confuse schmoozing someone on the phone with actually having a relationship with them.

Meeting people face to face is the ONLY way to develop a relationship. (Alright, I know that there are thousands of saddos out there who have "relationships" with people via various whacked dating websites. But what I'm saying is that for a relationship to thrive and prosper, you're going to have to spend some time in the other's company. Lovely though all those emails and phone calls may be, they're not in the same league as seeing someone in person.)

As a general rule of thumb, face to face always trumps the Silver Tongue. I wish executives would remember this.

On *The Sun*, I'd occasionally be out in the field endeavouring to buy up some punter's story. And inevitably, just as you'd reached the critical point of the charm offensive, your phone would ring. It would be one of the mad-masters, and they'd "helpfully" say, "Let me speak to the punter".

Now I'm fully aware that mad-masters can be not too bad with the Silver Tongue; one deputy editor was oral hair-oil. But for an executive to think that he can be more charming on the phone than a reporter who's actually there in the house…

Are they losing their marbles?

So, if it's a buy-up or it's generally important that you get someone on side, then it HAS to be done face to face.

This was all brought home to me a few months ago, when I was in the luxurious position of having two separate lots of film-people stalking around one of my novels. For five years, there hadn't been a sniff of interest in the book and then suddenly, within days, these two guys both wanted to buy the rights.

Terrific!

One of them was an accountant whom I'd met on holiday four years earlier. I liked him, but I hadn't seen him since and had only really spoken to him once on the phone. We'd exchanged a number of chatty emails.

The second guy was a young man. Also greatly enthused by the project.

But the difference was that the second guy flew up to Edinburgh. Just to see me. And there exerted his considerable charm skills.

I was bowled over.

Guess who got the deal.

The Silver Tongue is ideal for doing the groundwork; for teeing everything up; for getting someone generally on side.

But do not ever think of it as a means of forging a relationship.

You are only properly connected with someone if you have personally met them. Over a coffee. Over lunch. I don't care, just so long as you are able to look them in the eyes. (Skype? Are you having me on?)

SUPERSTITIOUS

I may have mentioned it before - and I'm damn well going to mention it again. Red Top readers have a number of buttons that need to be regularly pressed. Some buttons - like sport, humour, showbiz, and perhaps even tits and bums - need pressing every day. There are other buttons, which also need to be pressed fairly regularly.

Superstition is a very strange one. The thrill of the weird and the supernatural may vary from country to country, but you want to be aware that, for many Red Top readers, superstition can be a very powerful button.

It's not that they necessarily believe in all these strange supernatural goings-on. They don't necessarily disbelieve them either. But they're very intrigued. They want to know more.

In America, the big supernatural themes might include Big Foot, Vampires and Zombies. In the UK, Red Top readers *love* reading about UFOs and wild beasts roaming about wind-swept moors and, always, the Loch Ness Monster. In Africa, there is huge interest in magic, spirits of the ancestors, and an all-powerful bogeyman, the Tokoloshe.

On South Africa's *Daily Sun*, stories about the Tokoloshe are generally the biggest sellers by far. Readers can't get enough of them.

But the problem facing the editor is that although he gets plenty of reader ring-ins with strange Tokoloshe stories about beds miraculously being transported onto roofs, how can he dispassionately report these stories whilst at the same time purporting to be a genuine newspaper?

A Red Top newspaper needs to be fairly objective about its news-stance, otherwise it can soon turn into a joke.

When it first started ten years ago, *The Daily Sun* would regularly report these bizarre Tokoloshe stories as if they'd actually happened. The publisher, Deon Du Plessis contended that if somebody actually believed that some magical event had occurred, then it was the paper's perfect right to print the story as fact.

Hmmm.

So why not go off to the lunatic asylum and start interviewing all the people who think they're Napoleon Bonaparte?

Deon soon realised the flimsiness of his position and his paper backed off from reporting Tokoloshe stories as fact.

But was there, I wondered, another way of giving Red Top readers their fill of the superstitious without putting it into news stories? Well as it happens…

If your readers *really* love superstition, then you should think about having a weekly column. Let's call it "Little Miss Superstitious". Miss Superstitious can report all the good stuff that's coming in every week, as well as all the magical goings-on from around the world, whilst at the same time being able to take a step back from the news. At the end, say, of a story of a possessed chicken, Little Miss Superstitious can finish off by giving a wink to the readers. That's not to say she's taking the piss out of the story, but she is being ever so slightly sceptical.

Another way to get more magic into the Red Tops. Damn simple this one, and it works EVERY time. Buy up the rights to a big-selling book on the supernatural. Serialise it every day. If you really wanted to push the boat out, you could get a few pictures drawn up to go with the story.

Some Red Top executives make the error of getting an in-house writer to do up the story and do the pictures. Invariably it fails, because the in-house writer doesn't really know what he's doing, doesn't know what buttons he should be pressing.

With this sort of thing, there is absolutely no point in trying to reinvent the wheel. There are HUNDREDS of books already out there which have a proven track record and which the Red Top readers have been devouring for years. These are the stories that you want to be buying up. These are the stories that you want to be serialising.

You might think that Red Top readers in the West are immune to stories of magic and superstition. But you would be wrong.

Take a look at the astrology columns. Most people don't believe in that star sign nonsense, but they'll still be looking up their horoscope every day. And if you serialised a book on, "Your star sign, your love life," they'd be reading every word of it.

Second… Ah yes! This story is absolutely extraordinary. I've been saving it up. It's a real gem.

A little agency story had come through to the *Sun* news desk about a house fire. It said that an entire house had gone up in smoke. Everything had been torched, save for a picture above a mantelpiece, which had miraculously remained unharmed. This was a picture of a Crying Boy and it was to be the start of a story that has gone down in Fleet Street history.

At the end of the six-par story, the agency reporter had added one last throwaway line. She wrote, "Some people say there is a curse attached to the Crying Boy picture."

Kelvin MacKenzie was the editor at the time. He was a total despot, mad, mercurial and also, on occasion, utterly brilliant.

MacKenzie knew all about the Crying Boy pictures. They usually comprised a pseudo-oil painting of some waif-like five-year-old with two fat tears on his wan cheeks.

They also happened to be extremely popular with Britain's blue-collar workers.

The next day: Ba-Ba-Boom! It's all over *The Sun*'s front page - "The Curse Of The Crying Boy". And, included at the end of the story was - crucially - a Come-On, asking the paper's 10 million readers if they had also suffered from the Curse of the Crying Boy.

They most certainly had. The story ran for days and days, with ever more lurid tales of the disasters that had been caused by the cursed picture.

It was what happened next that, for me, turned the story into the truly surreal. Over the next week, the tone of the readers' calls started to change.

Many of them were now very concerned about their Crying Boy pictures. Was there, perhaps, any way that the curse could be lifted?

Not a problem, said *The Sun*. Send your Crying Boy pictures in to us.

And they did.

The saga ended when the reporter Paul Hooper was promoted for the day to "Fine Arts Correspondent" and then despatched off to a dump to burn all the wretched pictures that had been sent in.

How many Crying Boy pictures were there? *Tens* of thousands, enough to fill two articulated lorries.

Still reckon that Red Top readers aren't interested in superstition?

AND YET MORE EXCLUSIVES...

In most newsrooms in the morning, you'll find the reporters loafing around waiting to be sent off on a story. There they sit, flicking through the papers as they dismally wait for the phone to ring. Some of them even have the nerve to do their expenses in the office. This is a very, very bad idea. News editors do not like to see their minions toiling away at their expenses when they should be damn well digging up stories.

The problem though for a new reporter on the paper is that the phone *isn't* going to ring. You probably don't have a contact to your name - and any contacts you do have, you've already called twice in the previous week, just to check if they've got anything new for you. Surprise, surprise, they have not.

So what do you do next?

I was faced with this particular problem when I started shifting on *The Sun*. What news editors want to see as they gaze at their serried ranks of reporters is hacks hitting the phones; pumping people for stories; bringing in the goods.

What they do not want to see is you having another cup of coffee as you leaf through another paper that should have already been read before you even entered the office.

So if you haven't got any contacts, you've got to *make* them.

What sort of contacts do you want to have?

Very simple: people who can give you stories. Not just people who can give you stories, but people who actually know what a story is.

Unfortunately - as we know - punters wouldn't know what a story is unless a plane actually exploded above their heads.

But there is one much maligned breed that *does* know what a story is, and what I'm suggesting is that you make it your business to become their best buddy.

I'm talking about the PRs.

Here's how it worked for me. In Britain, there was a magazine called *Press Gazette*. (Now online.) In the back of it were the numbers of hundreds of PRs who were doing the publicity for everything from the AA to Cadbury's chocolate.

One by one, I systematically started calling up every single PR firm. (Very good way to practise the Silver Tongue, by the way.) If there was nothing going on in the office, there I'd be on the phone, ploughing through all the PRs. I'd always try and target the boss, which is usually much more productive than dealing with the underlings.

After about fifty calls, I'd developed quite a good patter. It went something like this, "Hi, Bill Coles here from *The Sun* newspaper - bit of a low news day at the moment. Just wondered if you'd got much going on; if you'd heard of anything weird or quirky… "

From the other end of the phone, I would generally hear this sort of clunking noise; that would be the sound of the PR boss' jaw hitting the floor.

Think of it, for the first time ever, a genuine Red Top hack is calling them up, saying that there's a whole load of free space in the paper to promote their product.

What you may not appreciate, when you start working on a Red Top, is that you have immense clout. PRs, in particular, will perform cartwheels to get their festering products into your paper. That's why they send out all those tons of unreadable Press Releases. So to have a charming Red Top reporter call up and say, "Please let me puff your product"… They can't believe it!

After your charming intro, the PR boss will probably say that he's got nothing for you right now, but he'll have a think. Suggest he calls round all the regional managers; gets them to recall any funny or quirky story that they might have regaled to their colleagues in the pub.

Leave the PR boss your mobile number. (Not your work number, unless you're staff - otherwise somebody else will try and bag the story.) Proceed onto the next PR's number.

On a good day, you might make 30 or 40 calls. Two days later, you call up the tastiest ones. The ones who sounded like they were up for it. And all you do is just give the tree another charming little shake just to see what might fall into your lap.

With me, I generally found that about one in ten calls paid off.

But I was lucky enough to have one beauty of a story come in on the very first day - and that's when I saw the light.

I'd called up the AA, the car repair people, and by chance they happened to have a story in that morning. A guy with a false leg had pulled into a service station with a broken-down engine, and also a dodgy leg.

The driver called out the AA. The serviceman mended not only his car but his leg too. The story had Page Three lead written all over it.

Within the week, I was offering about four stories a day to my mad-masters, all of them having been lovingly provided by my new best friends, the PRs.

It goes without saying that once a PR has provided you with a story, you have to meet them. You don't own a PR until you have bought them lunch, gone out for a drink, and generally charmed the pants off them. You want to be in such a snug position that it's them who are calling *you* up with all their juicy exclusives.

Too many hacks forget that it is still essential to actually meet up with their contacts. Today, it's just too easy to keep in touch by calling people on the phone or sending emails or text messages. These all have their uses, but the essence of grooming a contact is that you have to meet them face to face, shake them by the hand, look them in the eye, and buy them a meal. And this, by the way, needs to be done periodically. At least once every six months. If you've got a good contact, you should be meeting up regularly, nurturing that relationship, so that in time they become a mate. These are the people who are going to deliver for you.

In many countries, there is no helpful list of contact numbers for all the main PRs. In this case, all you need to do is a little groundwork beforehand.

First of all, list the top 50 products that your Red Top readers are interested in. This might be Stella Artois, Domestos detergent and Renault cars. Then, via the internet, find out who the PRs are; schmooze accordingly.

Two rich seams tend to be travel companies and bookmakers. The travel companies tend to have a lot of good holiday stories (and may yet give you a load of freebies); the bookies will have the stories about weird bets and breathtaking accumulators.

SHOWBIZ

When it comes to showbiz, all normal newspaper rules go out the window. Stars are a very strange breed, and the only thing that the A-listers have in common is that they are all completely whacked. Have to be. Almost by definition. If they're *that* driven and *that* hungry to succeed, then there must have been one hell of a lot of weird stuff going on in their childhood.

This, however, is possibly not the best place to be airing my views on our current crop of celebs.

But if I could generalise, very roughly, I would say that dealing with stars is a pretty good nightmare.

You're either dealing with the stars who are on the way up and will do absolutely *anything* for publicity. (Bedding an already established star? It's only the oldest trick in the book.)

Then, on the flipside, you've got those Titans who *have* actually made it, and who seem to spend most of their time moaning about how they can't set foot on the streets without being papped on a mobile phone.

Generally, for us Red Tops, we're only interested in the A-listers, those glamour-pusses who are right at the very top of the tree, and unfortunately these days, our access to these superstars is very, very limited.

We are confined to those soulless junkets, where bored-out-of-their-minds stars wander from table to table, spouting claptrap to the showbiz reporters who are "lucky enough" to have received an invite.

If you're on a red hot Red Top, then you might even get 15 minutes all by yourself with the star - with just a single Rottweiler PR for company.

It's all pretty tough going. Doesn't matter what you ask them, the stars have always heard the question before. They're invariably bored. And if you do manage to slip in a good question, the PR will have stepped in before the star has even opened her mouth.

However...

Here are some thoughts.

If you're interviewing a star, it goes without saying that you need to have read *all* of the cuttings beforehand. This can sometimes give you a nice line of attack. Something that might just bear fruit. Possibly.

Kate Muir, the chief film critic of *The Times*, had an astonishing result at the Cannes Film Festival and with one single question managed to get the Danish director Lars von Trier thrown out of the festival. What a coup!

Before the press conference for von Trier's new film *Melancholia*, Kate had immersed herself in the director's cuttings. She had been particularly struck by some off-beat comments that he'd made about the Nazis in the Danish Film Institute magazine. (And if you're a tabloid hack and a celebrity starts making off-beat comments about the Nazis, then big, BIG alarm bells should be ringing.)

Kate cast a well-judged fly over von Trier's nose. She asked him about his admiration for the "Nazi aesthete".

Von Trier went off on one.

"I understand Hitler," he said. "I think he did some wrong things, but I can still see him sitting in his bunker at the end. He's not what you would call a good guy, but I understand much about him and I sympathise with him a little bit."

Von Trier went on to admire the Nazi architect Albert Speer - "one of God's best children" - before closing his speech with the words, "Okay, I'm a Nazi!"

A few hours later, von Trier tried to wriggle out of it in the only way he could: he blamed Kate. He said she'd stitched him up. What utter poppycock. The only thing Kate was guilty of was being a consummate pro and doing her homework. Personally, I'd have given her Journalist of the Year.

In celebrity interviews, you could do worse than trying what I like to call, "Route Superlative".

You're going to ask a whole load of questions that start, "What was the best... " or "What was the worst... "

Such as: "What was the worst holiday/dinner/date/car/husband that you've ever had?"

Or, if they need jollying up: "What was the best kiss/breakfast/apple/house/sex that you've ever had?"

Getting the picture? What you're trying to do is wake them up, shake them out of the boring railroad tracks that they are running on. You are trying to ask them a question, perhaps a nice question that they may not have considered before.

For me, I really hit pay dirt when I asked a star, "What was the most irresponsible thing you've ever done?" Because for true irresponsibility, you need to be not just jeopardising your own life, but also those of young children.

If you can get enough of these "superlative" answers, you've probably got a stand-alone column. Call it, "The Superlative Column" - run it every week. Might work.

One other thing to try with celebrities, and indeed sports stars. This can work very well if you are an executive who has at her beck and call lots and lots of reporters who are constantly interviewing stars.

This is how it works. During the interview, you're going to be teasing away at all the normal lines. You're going to be exploring anything that might have come out of the cuttings; you might, if you can get away with it, try Route Superlative.

Then... halfway through the interview you're going to ask three very, very easy questions. They might be, "What's the best Christmas present you've ever had?" and "What was your most memorable Valentine's Day", and you could cap it off with, "What's the best thing you gave your mum on Mother's Day?" Easy, eh?

Well, you might get some good answers, you might not.

But what if... when you came back to the office to write up your interview, you put the answers to these three questions into three special files. Let's call them the Christmas File, the Valentine's File and the Mother's File.

Then... well let's just suppose that in the course of the year, your team had interviewed 250 stars. That'd be just five a week - easy!

Are we there yet?

When it comes to Christmas Day, or Valentine's Day, or Mother's Day, you have now got enough exclusive material for a splash and a four-page spread, as all these stars spill their guts on what was their favourite Christmas present ever. This sort of information is impossible to get on a ring-around. No star worth their salt is going to bother telling you about their favourite Christmas present.

But if you're interviewing them anyway, then why not toss in these three little questions.

All it needs is a little bit of commitment from the executives. Just kick around a few reporters who have failed to ask the three questions - *pour encourager les autres*.

But of course if it's part of your job to mingle with celebs or sports stars, then it can be *you* who has your own three stock questions - and it'll be you who, come Christmas, brings in this stonking great exclusive.

These are the sort of reporters that editors like on their team. These are the sort of story-generating reporters who editors hate to see poached. And these are the sort of reporters who are going to end up earning a ton of money.

AND MORE SHOWBIZ...

When I worked on *The Sun*, my friends would often ask me about the celebrities I'd interviewed.

They would be suitably impressed when I told them.

Though by any stretch of the imagination, it would be difficult to describe what I did as "interviewing".

The technical term for it is "fronting up" - and for a few years I did rather a lot of it.

But rather than generalise about what happened, I will describe a typical incident. I was in New York. Elton John had had a stormy break-up with his manager, John Reid. I was sent off to have a polite word with Elton to see what he had to say on the matter.

Eventually, I managed to track him down to the Lincoln Centre where he was going to be performing that night.

Two hours waiting at the stage door with Shannon, my photographer. The rain is absolutely tipping it down.

A motorcade pulls up. The place is swarming with bodyguards who form a phalanx around the stage door. Elton's cheery face pops out of the black stretch limo. He's bustling towards the door - fast. I only had about two seconds. There was no time for a formal introduction.

"Elton!" I said. "You must be devastated about John Reid!" Elton did not break stride for even one moment. He turned his head. And, at the absolute top of his voice, he screamed into my face, "Fuck Off!"

Yes indeed, that's how it is with me and celebrities. There's never been any soft-soaping. All they ever do is swear at me. Chris de Burgh, he was another one. Remember him? He was the diminutive "Lady in Red" singer who was dubbed "Lady in Bed" by *The Sun* after he was caught bedding his nanny.

The first time that I had to front Chris up, I would say that he was a little vexed. But a year later, when I had to do it a *second* time after Chris had been caught with the self-same nanny, I think it would be fair to say that Chris was apoplectic. At first he didn't recognise me. And then he did recognise me. Perhaps it was my cut-glass accent that had given me away. "It's you!" he shrieked. "I'm so angry, I... I could hit you!"

Yes, please! The whole place was absolutely swarming with *Sun* photographers and if Chris had hit me, we'd have been all over the front page. Besides, how bad could it be getting hit by Chris de Burgh? (Oh, and on a different tack altogether: how on *earth* did Chris manage to sire a beauty like the former Miss World Rosanna Davison? Must have been a throwback. It's the only explanation.)

Anyway, after that pleasant little meander down memory lane, I have yet more useful tips about celebrities - and how to deal with them.

If you're in the showbiz trade for any length of time, it will not be long before a star hits on you and wants to sleep with you.

I'm not saying this is a bad idea. Plenty of stars end up marrying journalists.

But what I am saying is that you want to make them work for it. If they're a big star, then they'll have thousands of groupies wanting to sleep with them; groupies who'd do *anything* to sleep with them.

You, however, are going to make things just that little bit more difficult. You're a hack, a Red Top hack, and you're going to set yourself way, way apart from the run-of-the-mill groupies.

My general rule of thumb is that you don't bed a star unless they've taken you out for at least six - yes SIX - dates. I know it's going to be tough. But I promise you it'll be worth it in the long run. Are you in it for the long haul or just for the quick buck?

The key to cracking a celebrity is, I'm afraid, their PR. Now the A-listers are already going to have a lot of very heavy-hitting PRs who will already have their favourite tame hacks. It's not easy to try and break into this elite group of people. They've got their pet hacks who write whatever they tell them; why do they need to start courting somebody like you?

So instead, try and cultivate the PRs of the B-list and C-list stars who are on their way up. These are the people who are desperate to get into the newspapers. With luck, they might go all the way and you want to be sure that it's you who's clinging onto their coat-tails.

Middle-ranking celebrities have a slightly flexible relationship with the truth - in so far as they are usually prepared to say or do almost anything in order to get onto the front page. Take the PRs out for a drink and kick ideas around. Be creative. A starlet sleeping with an A-lister is so commonplace now that it's no longer news. But, say, a story that an actress was so keen on sculpting that she was going in for the Turner Prize... with a nude sculpture of herself... well that might just possibly make the Red Tops.

It goes without saying that your ultimate goal is to forge a personal relationship with the star herself - so that rather than having to go through the conduit of the PR, you can call up the star in person. Going to take a lot of time though that one.

One thing that can work quite well in interviews, especially celebrity interviews, is... The Final Question.

You've had your interview. The whole thing's over. You've shaken hands, you've said your goodbyes, and you've even pretended to turn off your tape-recorder. Then, when you're at the door, and their guard has come crashing down, you throw in one last question - but this is the absolute stinger. The one you've been dying to ask all along. "So tell me," you ask, cheery-like, "why did your wife finally kick you out?"

The master of the "false exit", as it's known, was not actually a journalist but a TV detective - Columbo, played by Peter Falk. Columbo would be almost out of the door before he'd turned and say, "Just one more thing". The line was so famous that it became his catchphrase.

Save your nastiest question for when you're walking out of the room. You never know, you might even get a truthful answer.

AND SHOWBIZ PICTURES

Rear-Admiral Grace Hopper: not just a computer pioneer, but also the man who coined a phrase that should be the personal motto of every Red Top hack in the business.

"If ever you have a good idea, then you should act on it immediately - because it's much easier to apologise than it is to ask for permission."

Meaning?

What that means is that, on a job, you never, never, NEVER ask for anyone's permission. Just do it. Feel like wandering onto a crime scene? Want to interview some star witness? Want to take a picture?

Then JUST DO IT!

Who knows what's going to happen next. You did something without permission! Maybe they won't even notice what you've done. Maybe they will. Maybe there's going to be a frank and forthright exchange of views.

This is not a problem! All you have to say is - and repeat after me - "Oh, I'm sorry."

Works pretty well. If you want, you can lay it on even thicker. How about, "Oh, I'm *terribly* sorry. I just didn't know!" (And stick that in your pipe and smoke it.)

What are they going to do now? You've apologised for whatever you've done. Well they can carry on belly-aching, but you've already got what you've wanted.

If you hang around and wait to ask for permission, then it's just too damn easy for the flunkies to say, "No!". Then you're really snookered, as you can no longer now feign ignorance.

Which brings me onto celebrity pictures. If you want to make it as a showbiz hack and "the person who knows the stars", then you can't just be getting the interviews with the stars. You've also got to be pictured with them - photographic proof that you genuinely are best pals.

This technique was pioneered by Piers Morgan when he was on *The Sun*. Good old Piers.

First: get your photographer in position - a few yards in front of the celeb.

Then: just go up to the celeb. Sit down next to them. Stand next to them.

Last: put your arm round the celeb. Smile for the camera with your "new best friend".

And if it all kicks off? "Ohhh… I'm *terribly* sorry… "

Do you think you'd have got that picture if you'd meekly gone up to the star and asked, "Would it be okay if I had my picture taken next to you… "?

COCK-UPS

I'll try and describe the exact feelings that you experience when you realise that the shit is in the process of hitting the fan - and that there are, perhaps, certain flaws associated with one of your stories.

The shit hitting the fan can manifest itself in a number of ways. It can be the stroppy phone call; or the solicitor's letter; or the writ. The writ is generally bad news. Solicitors' letters matter not one jot; we laugh in the face of solicitors' letters. But if you've got a writ, then they mean business.

So here's what happens. On *The Sun*, where these skirmishes were a fairly common event, it would normally begin with a mad-master coming over with the complaint/writ. He would then politely ask for your full thoughts in a memo.

You'd mouth some platitude and then - and I can still vividly remember it - the hairs would start to rise on the back of your neck. It was like a dog's hackles rising as it gets its first whiff of danger. I could feel the hairs prickling against my collar. And then, or so I'm told, I'd go absolutely white.

And what I'd be thinking is, "How bad is it? How deep am I in? Do I have a tape-recording?" And one more thing: "Is there any wriggle room here?"

I would then generally be left to my own devices. After skimming through the complaint, I'd call up the original story just to check what I'd originally filed. Sometimes you might be able to shaft one of the subs. Didn't happen often though. *The Sun* subs were pretty damn good; they really knew how to cover themselves.

In particular, I'd be checking to see how close I'd been sailing to the wind or to see if the story had been "stretched", of which more later.

Next, I'd check my notebook and start searching desperately for "the" tape. Do yourself a favour and start dating all tapes and notebooks as a matter of course.

Some general rules for cock-ups: do not be rushed into giving your explanation.

Get your story right and then stick to it. Never use the word, "Assume", as it is guaranteed to have a mad-master foaming at the mouth.

If there's been an error with a story, the initial complaint may well come to you via a phone call. Never admit liability, the call is probably being taped.

If you can, stick the words "without prejudice" into the conversation.

Get them to put the complaint in writing to the boss.

It can sometimes work to call the complainant back five minutes later. Tape the conversation. Here's what you say, "Now what was all that about you wanting an apology? I didn't quite understand what the problem is. I thought you said that… "

If you catch them with their guard down and you're acting hurt and bewildered, you can sometimes get them to admit that they're only complaining because their client has kicked up a fuss. But you can't waste time to make these calls. They have to be done quickly before the complainant has become entrenched in his position.

STORY STRETCHING…

A lot of worthy broadsheet readers imagine that most tabloid stories are total inventions.

Twenty years ago, this used to occur much more frequently, especially with showbiz stories. But these days, most Red Top stories are absolutely copper-bottomed. If a story is truly shocking or scandalous, then it will most assuredly be correct to the last detail; there are a lot of libel lawyers out there who would be only too pleased to sue the shirt off a Red Top editor.

Showbiz stories, however, are of a different category altogether. Showbiz reporters frequently connive with celebrity PRs to dream up any sort of confection that might make it into the front pages.

An example, that legendary *Sun* headline: "Freddie Starr Ate My Hamster". Freddie, surprise, surprise, did *not* eat anybody's hamster.

Another one from the mists of tabloid time? How about David Mellor's affair with Antonia de Sancha in which, famously, he had sex while wearing a Chelsea strip. Even at the time, it sounded a little implausible and that of course was because the whole line had been concocted by the celebrity PR Max Clifford.

The wannabe stars are still inventing their tabloid tales, and calling up their favourite picture editors to alert them to their latest hush-hush assignation.

Outside showbiz, however, it's rare to see a completely fabricated story.

What happens instead is that stories are "stretched". Not that we're making up the facts, or the quotes. But, perhaps, we are accentuating certain aspects of a story.

The thing is that a story is like a piece of elastic. It can be stretched and stretched. But eventually you reach a stage where - "Twang!" - the elastic snaps.

The first time I really came across it was in 1994 when I'd just become a *Sun* staff reporter. At the time, Prince William was a new boy at Eton, where I happened to have a number of contacts. These juvenile entrepreneurs kept me supplied with a fund of front pages, because although *The Sun* could not run any stories on Prince William, we filled our boots on tales about his tearaway chums. There's nothing that *Sun* readers like more than to read about toffs behaving badly.

One of my best contacts was an Etonian called Agent Orange. I never knew his real name. One day, he called up to tell me that two Eton boys had been arrested in the grounds of Windsor Castle; they'd been drinking.

I checked the story out and got the usual "No comment" quote from the school. I wrote it up. At best, I thought it might make a page lead. A couple of drunk Etonians getting caught in the grounds of Windsor Castle? Didn't sound like much of a story to me.

It was about 4pm in the afternoon - fairly late, by *Sun* standards. Most stories had to be filed by 3pm.

Neil Wallis, the mercurial Deputy Editor, was standing by the news desk, and he calls out across the newsroom, "Here Nelly! Can you have a go at re-writing this?"

Nelly Lazzeri has been tasked with rewriting my story. I look over her shoulder as she tapped away at her keyboard. Such a simple little twist. She had transformed it into a World Exclusive Splash.

Here, as I remember it, is what she wrote: "Two drunk Etonians were arrested in Windsor Castle last night - on their way to see the Queen."

On their way to see the Queen?? I still have no idea where that one came from, but it was ingenious. Materially, it didn't alter the story in the slightest. But from a story point of view, it changed everything.

Another example of story-stretching. Certain names are going to have to be changed, for this particular scamp has now become one of the mad-masters.

It was about eighteen years ago and the London mobster Ronnie Kray had finally died in Broadmoor Hospital. This was quite a big story for the Red Tops as even though Ronnie and his twin brother Reggie had been locked up for over thirty years, the pair still held an incredible mystique.

Squads of *Sun* reporters were despatched all round London; and, just for old time's sake, a reporter was sent off to Broadmoor. Let's call this reporter Alfie.

Broadmoor is one of Britain's most secure psychiatric hospitals, and is home to some of Britain's most notorious criminals, including the Yorkshire

Ripper, Peter Sutcliffe. Not all that easy to get out of Broadmoor, not at all easy to get in to it, either.

This detail did not stop Alfie from getting an exclusive chat with a "nurse" who'd overheard Ronnie Kray's final words as he'd breathed his last. Apparently Ronnie - who was very close to his mum Violet - had been heard whispering, "Mother, I'm coming to you."

Hmmm.

I happened to be on the news desk that day when this mildly astonishing piece of copy came over. Some eyeballs were rolled.

Perhaps it is just the blurring of the mists of time, but I think I can even remember one of the news editors saying, "Christ, couldn't he come up with anything better than that?"

Didn't stop it from making the Splash though - and a world exclusive to boot.

We love celebrities' "last words". Let us just say that when a star has died, there is considerable scope for manoeuvre.

My general rule on stretching is that you do not want to go anywhere near story-stretching until you really, *really* know your stuff. You've got to have a lot of experience.

News editors are seeing hundreds of stories every day. They have this uncanny sixth sense that enables them to scent out a vaguely dodgy quote or a line that has been stretched.

AND WHEN COCK-UP TURNS
TO DISASTER

A cock-up turns into a disaster when the editor himself has to start eating Humble Pie.

Disasters stem from some catastrophic error of judgement. There are usually two causes.

The first is because the editor has turned into such a megalomaniac that he slaughters anyone who even remotely disagrees with him - to wit, that ranting despot at *The Sun*, Kelvin MacKenzie.

The second happens because an editor is so desperate to hang onto his world exclusive that not enough executives have been brought into the loop.

I believe that big stories should be examined by as many executives as possible. It's true that one genius is quite capable of producing a brilliant line or a brilliant headline. But the more people that are checking over a story, the more likely that every single nuance and ramification can be explored.

Some examples, the first one has, like many of MacKenzie's front pages, become the stuff of Fleet Street legend.

It was after the Hillsborough disaster when 96 Liverpool fans were crushed to death. At the time, there was a very febrile atmosphere in Liverpool. A lot of grief but no real focal point for the rage.

Britain's Red Tops had been attracting considerable anger after running with some quite graphic pictures of the disaster.

But it was *The Sun* that became the lightning rod for Liverpool's grief, and it was entirely the fault of Kelvin MacKenzie.

During his editorship of *The Sun*, MacKenzie had created an atmosphere within the newsroom that was nothing less than a complete Reign of Terror.

I had one friend who was a reporter for the paper at the time; he was quite a hard man. Sometimes he would be physically sick before he went into the *Sun* newsroom.

So when MacKenzie dreamed up his insane front page, there was not a person in the newsroom who dared take him on.

MacKenzie had decided to go with the police line that it was the Liverpool fans who were largely to blame for the tragedy. In particular, he had latched onto an agency report that claimed some fans had urinated upon the dead and looted their cash and jewellery.

He spent half an hour on the splash headline.

It filled almost half of the front page: "The Truth".

That day there was not a single executive who did not think that MacKenzie had taken leave of his senses. The story was nowhere near "The Truth"; it was merely the police's version of events.

But after years of bullying, they'd been so cowed that they all just shook their heads and knuckled under. No-one could tell MacKenzie that he was making a massive mistake.

Overnight, *The Sun* lost 250,000 readers and, even to this day, it has *never* got them back.

Another example of editors losing the plot?

For the first and only time that I can remember, *The Sun* newsroom went into near meltdown.

Normally, even with the biggest of stories and the tightest of deadlines, the newsroom sails on serene, as effortless as a swan gliding across a mill pond.

Not this day though. This day, *The Sun* had dropped one hell of a clanger. At about noon, a slight whisper came over the wires that all was not well with that morning's splash.

There'd been so much interest in the story that I, a humble reporter, had been drafted onto the news desk for the day. I guess I pretty much had a front-row seat.

Our splash, which was being followed up around the world, was of a grainy video of Princess Diana romping in a garden with her lover James Hewitt. At one stage she was even riding him like a horse. The video, or so we claimed, raised serious security issues.

The balloon went up at about lunchtime. The whole of the front page story was a fake. Worse than that, a few weeks earlier, our sister paper, the *News of the World*, had turned down the exact same video.

It all went rather quiet in the newsroom as we digested this unpalatable piece of news. I would not have liked to have been the person who'd told the editor.

Suddenly, reporters were being dispatched all over London. We were trying to launch a massive salvage operation. Above all, we were trying to find exactly what had gone wrong. *

But what had actually gone wrong was that not enough executives *were* in the know - and those executives that were in the know, were just desperate to believe that the story was true. As they tried to make the story work, they dropped all their natural scepticism.

Only a few days later did it become clear that the whole video was absolutely riddled with flaws. There were about a dozen giveaways, which revealed the thing to be a fake.

The cock-up occurred though because Stuart was desperate to hang onto his exclusive. (Though he was such a good sport about it that that Christmas, he parodied the story in *The Sun*'s Christmas card.)

Generally, the more executives who are being counselled on a splash, the better.

And as for the editors who act like tin-pot dictators, I think they are stark staring out of their minds. Of course, all the screaming and swearing may, in some small part, make up for their miserable marriages and their estranged children. But since today's Red Tops are primarily about ideas and creativity, then relentless bollockings are the very last way of getting the best out of a team.

I'm not saying that we don't have discipline. I love a tight ship. I do know that most Red Top reporters have a natural inclination to both deviousness and indolence. But the person who should be delivering these bollockings is not the editor, but the deputy, or an associate. The editor is the five-star general, warm and competent, and she leaves her bollockings to one of her minions.

A tyrant editor is just a disaster waiting to happen. He (and it's usually a "he") is so confident of his infinite talents that he probably believes he's never, ever made a mistake - and doubtless will still be continuing to believe in his own infallibility even after he's had to run yet another full front page apology.

* I had a personal hand in the follow-up to the Diana video fiasco.

I was kicked out of my snug billet on the news desk and sent haring off across London to interview the theatrical agent who was responsible for hiring out the two lookalikes for the video.

I strolled up the garden path, knocked on her door and gave the woman my most charming smile.

"I'm terribly sorry to bother you," I said. "Bill Coles from *The Sun*. My editor is ever so slightly concerned that he's been sold a pup."

She had this fixed smile. I absolutely knew something wasn't right. I couldn't tell what was wrong. But my intuition was blaring away at top volume.

I ignored it.

The woman, God rot her, fobbed me off and asked me to wait a couple of minutes on the doorstep.

Eventually, she let me in and we sat down at the kitchen table as she went through her spiel. She told me all about it.

The one thing she signally failed to mention was that she'd just been talking to a crew from the *Mirror* - and that the reporter had been hiding behind the front door when I'd knocked.

No - I only discovered this very minor detail the next day, when I saw that I'd been quoted, in full, by the *Mirror*.

Bastards. Very poor show from the agent. And very poor form from the *Mirror* reporter too, stiffing a rival reporter like that. I have not forgotten her.

But the biggest idiot of the lot was me. Right from the first, I'd sensed that something was wrong.

I didn't do anything about it.

Cultivate your intuition. Don't ask *why* your antennae are waving all those warning flags. Something's not right. So wake up! Pay attention! With the faked Diana video, there was a slight sense of uneasiness on *The Sun*. It was very difficult to put your finger on the problem. But the story just had a vibe that something wasn't quite right.

When you sense this intuitive vibe, then do not start searching around for reasons to validate it. Go with your gut.

SUBS - WE LOVE 'EM

It does not happen often. But I genuinely lost my temper.

It was quite a sight. Even four years later, they were still talking about it on *Die Son* in Cape Town.

Mad? I was incensed.

I am told that I was standing up, rocking back on my heels, and quite white with rage as I bawled out at the news team.

And it all started because I'd discovered that the news reporters had been berating the subs.

So let me make one thing quite clear: reporters should be getting down on their knees and licking the subs' boots in gratitude for what they do. The subs get none of the glory. They get no expenses. They get no fancy lunches. They don't even get the time to call up their mates.

It is true that sometimes, though not very often, they might do a piece of rewriting that makes your elegant prose sound slightly clunky.

But these are the wordsmiths who are preventing your grossest howlers from getting into the paper. And, for the most part, they are making your shit copy shine like diamonds.

That, my friend, is why you should be *extremely grateful* to these worker bees whose sole job is to polish up your lousy copy.

Therefore, it is completely unacceptable for a reporter to start berating a sub. You may not like what they've done with your beautiful pearls. But tough shit, my friend - soak it up.

Occasionally, you'll get a highly-paid columnist who can actually write and who will let off a bit of steam when their copy has been tampered with. I don't think it's professional behaviour, but if a columnist is being paid a ton of money, then they've got a few cards in their hand. Reporters, however, should be saying nothing whatsoever to the subs apart from a heartfelt "thank you".

Got it?

Which brings me back to the news team on *Die Son*.

Let me just say that their story-writing technique left a lot to be desired. Not to worry - I gave them a complete blueprint on how to write a Red Top story (See Appendix 1); and for those hacks who couldn't be bothered to read my blueprint, I'd even boiled it down to a ten-point guide.

In the usual hack fashion, the reporters ignored me.

Maybe it was because I'm English. Maybe it was because I was charmless. Maybe they didn't like the bolshy tone of my voice. Who knows? Maybe they all thought I should sod off and teach my grandmother to suck eggs.

So, like the stream that rolls relentlessly down the Highland Hills, I merely glided round the obstacle. Instead of trying to convert the reporters, I started singing my song to the subs, teaching *them* how to write a tabloid story.

Ah yes. I well remember what happened next.

As per my orders, the subs started totally rewriting the reporters' copy. It was lovely. For about one hour, I was very happy.

The one thing I hadn't expected was that the reporters would start *complaining* at how their pieces of odious shit were being polished up by the subs.

I had an absolute fit.

And that - if I were a news editor - is what I'd be doing with *any* reporter who took it upon themselves to criticise a sub. Maybe I'd even give the hack a written warning. Maybe I'd sack them. *Pour encourager les autres*. For let me tell you this about Red Top hacks: *les autres* tend to need plenty of *encouragement*.

Maybe it is in our nature, but Red Top reporters generally only give of their best when the mad-masters are wielding big carrots – and even bigger sticks.

TAPE RECORDING

There is one eternal truth about newspaper stories and that is that when a celebrity or a politician lands themselves in the mire through some injudicious comment, they will *always* say that they've been misquoted, or that the quote has been "taken out of context".

Well, I suppose that we hacks are occasionally guilty of misquoting celebs and that we may even take a quote out of context.

But we're in a much, *much* more comfortable position if we've got an actual tape-recording of the conversation.

So - this is what I want: in future, if there is any likelihood whatsoever that a person is going to claim that you've fabricated a quote, then it's up to you to have the thing on tape. For any interview with a weasel politician or a slippery celeb, then you've *got* to have it on tape - otherwise it's just too damn easy for them to say you've made the whole thing up.

Date the tapes and keep a meticulous log. About twice a year, you'll have to provide a transcript of a tape. It can really screw up your weekend if you're trying to retrieve a cassette from the 50-odd tapes that are strewn at random through your drawers.

On the *Cambridge Evening News*, we had a spruce young pup come to join the ranks of the news reporters. His name was Matt Dickinson and he was fresh out of the local University. His dream, he said, was to become a top-flight sports journalist, but first he wanted to be trained up as a news hound.

That he did, learning shorthand and covering the courts and the councils.

A few years later, Matt was a *Times* sports reporter, still yet to win his spurs but definitely well on the way.

That day was not long in coming. He was due to have a phone interview with Glenn Hoddle, the England football manager. Like any good news hack, he'd diligently gone through all the cuttings.

One thing, in particular, looked like it had possibilities. A few years earlier, Hoddle had alluded to some rather strange views on reincarnation.

Matt was having a shower when Hoddle called and so, with a towel around his midriff, he scribbled onto his notepad in his immaculate 100 words per minute Teeline shorthand.

For what Hoddle was saying was extraordinary. He more or less believed that the handicapped and the disabled are born that way because of something bad that they've done in a previous life.

I guess these sort of beliefs are fairly standard across broad swathes of America. But coming from the England football manager, it was nuclear-grade news.

As soon as the story hit the front page, Hoddle issued the classic double denial: quotes manipulated, quotes taken out of context.

For a while it worked. All Matt had to back up his interview was the miserable transcript from his notepad.

Who would crack first?

Hoddle kept his rear-guard action going for about a week, but eventually the Red Tops turned their fire on the England manager and Hoddle crumbled. He was out.

Scoop of the year. Sports journalist of the year. Matt's career went into orbit.

But I can tell you that he'd had a few sleepless nights over the lack of a proper tape-recording.

So, just for old time's sake, get yourself a little tape-recorder.

There's one other huge advantage to having an interview on tape. When it all kicks off and the writs start flying, your mad-masters can put the tape on one of their premium rate phone lines, better that your army of readers can hear the interview for themselves at the bargain price of 20 pence per minute.

(And if you've also got it videoed, you've got yourself a YouTube classic.)

TITS 'N' BUMS

Pretty girls are an essential part of the Red Top mix. Not - remotely - that they have to be topless. But most Red Top editors know that they have to have a healthy smattering of beautiful women in the paper. Perks the paper up, makes it more fun.

As a result, staff photographers need to be briefed much more tightly. When it comes to taking pictures, then Red Top photographers should ensure that there is a pretty girl up front and that her clothes are, for preference, tight and skimpy.

I had a small fit on *Sondag* newspaper in Johannesburg after reading a story about a beautiful woman who was biking round the whole of Africa. The photographer had thought fit to illustrate this story with a picture of the bike in the foreground and the woman wearing a very baggy grey jumper.

This is bonkers! Red Tops are certainly not obsessed with tits and bums, but we are aware that a pretty woman can shift a ton of papers - hence the reason why, for preference, we like to have a picture of a pretty woman on the front page.

Even the picture editors on the British broadsheets have got this point. And so, every year as our teenagers celebrate their A-level results, our newspapers invariably run with pictures of gorgeous young girls jumping for joy. (Spotty boys? Well they may well have got some good grades, but their jubilant faces will never be gracing the front page of a British newspaper.)

I'm also not suggesting that the whole of a Red Top is packed out with pictures of pretty women. In moderation. Everything in moderation.

Now - this business of having topless girls on Page Three. The concept was dreamed up by Rupert Murdoch and Larry Lamb when they relaunched *The Sun* in 1969 - and it's true that it all helped create the frothy, bubbly image of the *Soaraway Sun* that took its sales to over four million.

But there is a big problem with topless girls on Page Three: many people are always going to consider the paper to be inherently sexist and downmarket. It is also difficult to be taken for a heavyweight paper, as stories will often be perceived as flaky and sensationalist. Not that this is necessarily a problem - unless you want to shift your paper slightly upmarket.

Some years ago, the paper considered dropping its topless Page Three girls. The scheme was shelved after the mad-masters realised that they'd immediately lose about ten per cent of their readership. That's a hell of a hit for an editor.

So I'm not saying that Page Three is wrong. There are a lot of readers out there who, even in these days of free sex videos on the internet, will still buy a paper because it has a topless girl on Page Three. But it's important to be aware of the long-term ramifications.

Personally, I think that models should keep their clothes on. If a model is wearing a bra or a skimpy swimming costume, then the reader relies on his own imagination to fill in the blanks - and in his mind's eye, he will conjure up the fantasy girl of his own choice. This fantasy girl will - always and without exception - be far, far superior to the actual reality. Clothes on is far, far sexier for the readers. Bikinis are much more enticing than topless boobs.

One final question. Which edition of *Sports Illustrated* notches up its biggest sale of the year? It happens to be the "Swimsuit catalogue", with scores of utterly gorgeous supermodels. Every single one of them is - you'll never believe it - wearing either a bikini or a swimsuit.

THE BIG STICK

You've been dispatched over a hundred miles to interview some rogue politician who's been having an affair with his secretary. Given the current sexual climate, it's not exactly a huge story but it might make a page lead. Perhaps even a spread.

If you can get him to open up.

This will be unlikely even though you're going to be just as charming as you know how.

When charm fails - as I'm afraid it sometimes will - some reporters then decide to change tack. They start wielding the Big Stick. It's like they're dealing with a stubborn mule, and after the carrot has failed they start beating the beast with a bat.

This is a very bad idea.

I'll explain why.

In Red Top terms, the Big Stick invariably involves some sort of threat. It usually runs along the lines of, "There's a hard way and there's an easy way of doing this. But we're running this story tomorrow and unless you give me a comment you are going to be so totally screwed."

Well sometimes it works. But the point is that if it *does* work, the rogue politician is unlikely to want to start pouring his heart out to you. If there is going to be a full and frank interview, somebody else is going to have to do the job. This is not good.

It's a classic case of "Good Cop, Bad Cop". You need *two* people for the thing to work properly. If you have *one* person being alternately charming and menacing then the poor old interviewee will soon be running for the hills.

This is where your bosses, the mad-masters, come in. As already discussed, bosses are notoriously *bad* at winning punters round when you're in the field. Every time they call up, they invariably come within an inch of screwing things up.

But the one thing that the mad-masters are very *good* at is playing the part of the bad cop. Guess they've got quite a lot of experience.

So if there are threats to be made, then get someone else to do the dirty work. You, however, are just going to continue to tap into that pit - that bottomless pit - of charm. That way, when your punter finally agrees to the chat, you can just roll your eyes at the blunt tactics of your pit bull colleague.

At the end of it all, it's got to be you doing the interview. That being the case, it should never be you who makes the threats.

(I'm reminded about the great line from the Labour heavyweight, Alan

Johnson: "We launched a charm offensive. I was charming; he was offensive.")

AND CELEBRITY EXCLUSIVES...

I've always had a bit of a soft spot for Ivana Trump ever since I shared a burger with her in the back of a stretch limo in Manhattan.

At the time, Ivana had famously divorced Donald Trump, coining the sublime quote, "Don't get mad, get everything." She was in her fifties, single, and fantastically good fun. She also happened to have a slight predilection for young men...

Someone, somewhere, had dreamt up a stunt for a new product she was promoting. It was a new kind of burger, The Tower Burger, and for the purposes of the stunt, Ivana and I were going to be having a date in her private limo; further to that, I'd be treating her to one of those oh-so classy Tower Burgers.

The spread worked brilliantly. Lovely pictures of Ivana leaning out of the limo door as she accepted her burger. Lovely copy too: "Forget dinner in The Plaza, all I want is my Tower Burger - and you."

Perhaps I should have asked her for a date later that evening. I was certainly young enough. But I don't think it would have worked. I didn't spend nearly enough time in the gym.

Some thirteen years later, and I'm talking to the hacks in South Africa when one of them, Mashoto, comes up with a brand new idea. Here it is.

Red Tops should be making much, much use of the celebrities that are endorsing everyday products. If you've got an actor, a singer, or a sports star who is endorsing some food or beverage, then you should start dreaming up gentle ways to have some fun with them.

In Mashoto's case, there was a footballer in South Africa who was endorsing McDonald's. Mashoto had the star "working for the day" in McDonald's, flipping burgers before finally serving Mashoto with his very own Big Mac. Great pictures, great story. Both the footballer and McDonald's were happy and Mashoto's editor was also pretty damn happy at this funny exclusive.

If you're on a Red Top, then find out which of your readers' favourite products are being endorsed by celebrities. Then, over a couple of pints with the PRs, dream up a soft stunt that will get their product and their star into the paper. (And, once you've got them on side, then make sure you *keep* them on side by taking them out for dinner.)

AND MY LAST WORD ON FINDING EXCLUSIVES

One of the joys of working on a daily Red Top is that at the start of each new day, the decks have been swept clean. You may have been trounced that morning by the rival hacks, but who the hell cares, as today, now, is your chance to stick it right back to them.

It's very energising. The hacks are on this non-stop cavalcade, snatching up story after story like gannets in a shoal of mackerel. Who cares what's going to happen tomorrow? Somewhere in the world, there's going to be a story.

This also makes it a very hand-to-mouth existence. Hacks on the dailies are hopeless at strategy or planning ahead - Just Give Me My Story!

The result of which is that most Red Top hacks can't be bothered to follow up their own stories. Can't be bothered? It never even *occurs* to them to follow up their own stories.

If you want to bring in more exclusives, then have a file in your desk with all your old cuttings. Periodically have a little look through that file. And if you think that there might be more fruit on the tree, then just give the tree another shake: see if anything more will fall to the ground. This goes back to what I was saying about chasing anniversaries. It applies to your own stories as well.

This is so *simple*, because you have already done the main donkey-work for the original story - that is, you've got all the contact details and you've already sweet-talked the punters. All you've got to do - literally! - is to open your contacts book, find that number, and have a five-minute conversation. Then, as you polish your golden halo, you waltz over to the news desk and say, "Boss! You know that couple that had twenty-five children? Well guess what! She's pregnant with number twenty-six!"

Easy, eh? Well, my friend, it may seem easy, but I can promise you that very few Red Top hacks every bother to revisit their old stories. For them a story is just old news, and they're just too damn indolent or unimaginative to think that what seemed like a one-off bloomer may yet become a hardy perennial.

If we attack all stories with a view to being able to milk them many times over, it will also change our habits after a story has made it into print. This is a very good thing.

Most Red Top hacks could not care less about a story once it's made it into the paper. Unless there's a pressing need for a new line, then they wouldn't even *think* of calling up an interviewee to find out how they are and whether they're happy with the story.

This is what you need to start doing. When a story has appeared in the paper, call up the interviewee and spend three minutes - *three minutes!* - giving them a stroke and thanking them for their time. You want to be leaving the punters on really good terms. If needs be, send them a few copies of the pictures. True, it may take up all of 15 minutes of your time in the morning when you could be doing something infinitely more important like reading the papers and drinking coffee.

But these small acts of kindness are the key to making sure that any follow-ups come straight back to you. Christmas cards are another good idea. Most Red Tops produce their own Christmas cards. Doesn't cost you anything but a little bit of time. Send out cards to everyone who's helped you with a story in the previous year.

What most hacks forget is that being interviewed by a Red Top reporter and then featuring in a daily paper is, for many people, a terrifying experience. What do we care? We're already onto the next story. But if you - unlike all the rest of the pack - treat an interviewee with generosity, and if you bother to call up the next day to find out how they are, then when there is a follow-up, they might even take it upon themselves to phone *you* up with their exclusive new line.

It goes without saying that all - and I mean *all* - contact numbers have to be regularly updated into your contacts book, preferably electronically. Don't just put in their names and numbers, but put in the *date* of the story to remind you of any possible anniversary follow-ups. Add in a few mental jogs to help you remember who they are. That way, when you're doing a fresh story on lightning strikes, it will take you just five seconds to call up all the numbers of Britain's very own Mr Lightning Bolt.

PACK JOBS

I used to love working with the pack. Less work all round. We could all go off and have a decent lunch. No sweating around having to interview all the neighbours. Don't have to do anything much at all, actually, apart from loaf around on the doorstep and spend the next ten hours gossiping. And all done in the full and certain knowledge that you were unlikely to be stiffed by a rival's exclusive.

Many journalists outside Britain have not come across "Pack rules" before, but once it's explained to them, they love it. Pack rules make for a much more civilised way of life.

On even a medium-sized story, there might be five reporters from five different newspapers waiting on a doorstep. They will soon find that they can operate much more efficiently if they work as a pack so that one reporter covers the back and one the front, while the other three go off and have a cup of tea together.

But the rules of the Pack Job mean that you can't hold anything back. If you've had some tasty interview with a neighbour, or you've filched some crumpled letter out of a dustbin, then you've got to share it with the rest of the pack. Sounds pretty obvious, but there are still some reporters who don't get it, and who believe that "Pack rules" entails taking everything from the pack and giving nothing in return.

But nobody ever forgets. If you shaft the pack, then word gets round very fast that you're a double-dealer.

There is one breed of reporter who will *invariably* try to stiff the rest of the pack. These are the broadsheet reporters. You want to watch them.

In my experience, Red Top reporters generally behave like gents. They'll do everything they can to help out. That's because they know, for a certainty, that world exclusives may come and go, but being scooped by the opposition is guaranteed to send the mad-masters into orbit.

But seeing as the broadsheet hacks see so few genuine exclusives, they perhaps don't feel the need to alert the rest of the pack when they do actually come across one.

Fifteen years ago in Boston, America. It's a big story, the British nanny Louise Woodward is being tried for the murder of a young boy, and Her Majesty's press is there in force with a staff reporter from every single newspaper.

Lovely. Pack rules, chaps?

Of course.

Night in, night out, we'd all have dinner together, wolfing down lobster thermidor and soft shell crabs at the expense of our mad-masters. Now *that*, my friend, is one very good reason why it's worth joining our bizarre trade.

Then one night it turns out that *The Guardian*'s correspondent has managed to get an exclusive interview with Louise Woodward's parents. More than that, it's all over the paper's front page.

Suddenly all the phones are ringing. All the mad-masters are screaming. "Why the hell didn't you get this story?"

"Sorry," says the *Guardian* hack, whose surname is not unadjacent to my own, and who now happens to be the editor of a rather well-known glossy women's magazine in New York City. "I didn't think you'd want it."

Yeah, yeah, yeah.

So - pack jobs are wonderful as you will have infinitely more clout than if you're operating as a lone wolf. But it helps if you can trust the other hacks.

It goes without saying that you're going to behave like a gent, we're in it for the long haul! Don't necessarily trust the other hacks to behave so honourably.

One thing to watch for on pack jobs is when you're all sent home. You've spent a long and fruitless day on a doorstep and although you know your hero is stuck inside, he's refusing to come out and speak.

At the end of the day, the mad-masters tend to do this elaborate dance. They'll only call you off if the rival hacks leave too. Eventually, you all leave together with honours even.

Except there's going to be one hack who's sent back to the doorstep an hour later, just to have one last bite of the cherry. It can be surprisingly effective. Punters may not be prepared to talk to the whole mob, but if they're confronted by a lone reporter, then they may well open up.

If the mad-masters suggest you do this, then of course you've got to follow orders. But if you've been operating under pack rules, then in my book, if you get a hit, then you've got to let the rest of the pack know. Store up those favours!

Just don't expect the rest of the pack to be quite so considerate.

SUBS - WE STILL LOVE 'EM (EVEN THOUGH WE MAY HATE WHAT THEY DO)

While I'm on the subject of Louise Woodward, it reminds me of an incredible piece of chutzpah on the part of one nameless *Sun* sub. What happened was that somebody, some unknown somebody, monkeyed with my copy. Just pepped it up a little. I was left… slightly red-faced.

I was in the courtroom when Louise Woodward was found guilty of murder - and it was an electric experience. It was Hallowe'en 1997, the jury had given their verdict, the judge had left the room, and all we could hear was the sound of this young girl screaming. Screaming and screaming at the prospect of being locked up for the next twenty years of her life. Two of the guards were in tears. The hairs actually stood up on the back of my neck. I can't remember anything like it.

The next day, my maddest master, Neil Wallis, asked me to file a 2,000-word colour piece, recounting all the drama and the passion from the courtroom.

A 2,000-word colour piece? Just exactly my *forte*. I was licking my lips at the prospect.

After all of two minutes deliberation, I hit on this intro: "The sight of British nanny Louise Woodward buckling at the knees and begging for mercy made grown men weep."

Sets the right tone. Puts you in the middle of the action. Perfectly alright as an intro. I then went on with something like, "In an astonishing travesty of justice… "

Anyway I filed my story and then had to get on with the next bit of stuff, as they were pretty much clearing the first nine pages for all things Louise Woodward.

When the story appeared in the paper the next day, it went in pretty much verbatim. Except there had been some tinkering with the intro, which now read like this: "The sight of British nanny Louise Woodward buckling at the knees and begging for mercy made grown men weep. I know. I was one of them."

Hmmm. How the rest of the pack howled.

The intro was so unusual that it was quoted in *Press Gazette*, *Private Eye* and about four newspaper round-ups. And so, looking back, I guess that it was actually an improvement because it also put *me* dead centre in the middle of the action.

NO COMMENT

Very often as you're grilling a punter they will say, "No comment". They don't really know what "no comment" means, but they use the line because it's what they've heard in all the movies.

A few years ago, I used to like coming back at them with the snappy retort, "I'm not looking for a comment, I'm just looking for the facts." This was rarely effective. All it succeeded in doing was putting people's backs up.

A much better way to deal with this is to just carry on pressing ahead with your own line. You'll not be asking questions as such. You'll be empathising with whatever experience your punter has gone through. To someone listening in, it could almost sound like two separate conversations.

The basic principle is that, whether you're on the phone or on the doorstep, you are going to carry on talking - and talking - until the phone has been slammed down or the door has been shut in your face.

And, seeing as most people are far too polite to actually shut a door in a person's face, even that of a reptilian hack, this means that you can carry on chatting away for quite some time. Eventually, you may find that they start to crack.

An example. Let's suppose that a famous English football star, say, David Beckham, has just been sent off during the 1998 World Cup, thereby causing England to be knocked out of the championship.

You have been tasked to track down David's girlfriend, Victoria Adams,

Posh Spice, who, by a complete stroke of genius, you have worked out is staying at The Four Seasons in New York.

Call through to The Four Seasons. Ask for Victoria Adams. And amazingly, you're put straight through.

Now - a gatekeeper answers the phone.

"Hello?"

"Oh I'm sorry to bother you at a time like this, I wondered if Victoria was about." (NB, not "Posh Spice", just her first name. You're trying to sound like a concerned friend.)

"Who's speaking?"

"Bill." (At this stage, it would be an error to declare yourself because you'll just get the phone slammed down. But by just leaving your first name, then the gatekeeper may believe you're a mate.)

Sounds of scrabbling.

"Hello?" Jesus - you discover it's Posh herself! If you're not standing up already, stand up now. You're really going to need your wits about you.

"Oh, I'm so sorry to bother you at a time like this, it's Bill Coles from *The Sun*. I know you must be absolutely devastated by - "

"How the bloody hell did you get my number?"

"You must be devastated by what happened at the match tonight. Terrible, just awful." (Notice that: 1, you don't answer her question, and 2, you're not asking any questions yourself. With this sort of interview, you've got to keep talking, keep empathising.)

"You've got a bloody nerve calling me up at this time."

"It must have been terrible for you. And so unfair too, the way David got sent off for kicking that Argie… " (KEEP TALKING. THIS IS THE KEY.)

"No comment!"

"I couldn't bear to watch when he walked off the pitch. You must have been… "

Et cetera… Et cetera.

The point is about this ball-breaking conversation (which, of course, has been transcribed exactly) is that the hack has to keep pressing on. There is no let up. If the punter is a really cold fish, then you don't ask questions. You keep coming out with statements of empathy. If they agree, then you have at least got yourself a line or two of quotes that you can then put into the mouth of "a friend".

If, however, the punter is not a seasoned celeb, then - we hope - they will eventually start to warm to you.

So, never ever accept a "no comment" at face value. You are going to keep talking and talking until the phone is slammed down the hook. But don't ask questions. That's much too punchy. Be personable. Chatty. Emote. We are an unstoppable river, and we don't hit obstacles head on, we slip, we glide.

I'LL JUST PUT 'NO COMMENT'

-PILBROW-

YUK!

Yuk journalism is very simple: it involves a picture which makes the reader wrinkle up their nose in slight distaste and say the word, "Yuk!".

The operative words in that last sentence are "slight distaste". A picture is most definitely not "Yuk" if it makes a reader clutch at their eyes and say, "That is absolutely bloody revolting".

A subtle point? A grey area?

What we're talking about is the difference between pictures that are fit for a family newspaper, and sick photos that are beyond disgusting.

I know full well that repellent pictures can sell very well. In South America, there's an adult magazine that devotes itself entirely to these photos. Their perverse speciality is corpse photos, the more gruesome the death the better; some of the pictures are so strange they even border on the surreal. I particularly remember a picture of four decapitated heads in an ammunition box. It looked like a still life for the 21st Century.

The difference with Yuk pictures is that they may make you wince slightly, but they nonetheless hold a certain fascination. They're pictures that you wouldn't mind being seen by your nine-year-old son.

Yuk photos often involve people with gross disabilities - the obese, the deformed and the horribly injured. They can also involve people who've been in a horrific, yet slightly comic accident - SO LONG AS THEY HAVE SURVIVED. A burglar, say, who's slipped off a roof and impaled his leg on a fence post. A man who's got his head stuck in a gate. A woman with a javelin through her arm.

These are the photographic equivalent of the cringe-inducing films on YouTube where a man gets whacked in the privates by his infant son.

The difference between Yuk and Gore (which, as we know, Red Top readers also adore) is that Yuk is generally a picture, while Gore is described in words. It is true that a picture is sometimes worth a thousand words, but you *cannot* be using that picture if it's going to put people off their breakfasts. These are the times when less really is more - when it's far, far better to let the reporter do his stuff and capture the essence of what has happened with not a thousand, but one hundred well-chosen words.

Some examples from South Africa. A mother was doing her neighbour's hair and had left her two children playing at home. When she came back, both children had drowned in the pool.

What a horrific story.

A few minutes after the children had been dragged from the pool, the mother was photographed clutching one of the dead bodies. The picture was just awful.

One editor - a mid-market editor - decided to run with that photo. She justified it by saying that it would "teach parents not to leave their children alone next to a pool".

If I'd been the publisher, I'd have sacked her on the spot.

There are many other examples from South Africa where editors still can't distinguish between Yuk and Gore, and where newspaper sales are often the sole arbiter of whether a photo makes it into the paper.

I'm talking about a picture of a dead baby that had been abandoned on a town dump.

I'm talking about a picture of a dead boy on a pavement who has plunged ten-storeys.

These photos are just obscene; frankly, I think that if an editor can't tell when a picture is not fit for a family paper, then they shouldn't be in the job in the first place.

At the moment in South Africa, the Red Tops are – as in the UK – facing the distinct possibility of government action to control the country's thundering newspapers. Unless Red Top papers are brought to heel, and unless editors no longer run sick pictures just to score up a few more sales, then they'll only have themselves to blame when the government brings in new laws to control them.

AND MORE YUK!

Broadsheet papers, being papers of record and being largely read by adults, often spell out the most vile swear-words in full. *The Independent* prides itself on its use of the C-word. Well, good for them. I'm sure the readers just love to see the C-word in print as they're eating their cornflakes.

But it is entirely wrong for a Red Top to start spelling out expletives in full. Swear words take on a much greater power when they are in print. It's an even bigger blunder to use these words in a headline.

The reason - and I'm sorry, but I'm damn well going to reiterate the point - is that we are providing WHOLESOME FAMILY ENTERTAINMENT.

This means that we can have a slight bit of innuendo for the mums and dads, but we're not going to spell out all the graphic details of a star's extra-marital affair.

It means that - in general - our fairly conservative readers do not want to have blow-by-blow accounts of gay sex.

And it also means that if a star uses the C-word or the F-word, then we're going to have to spell it out as C*** and F***. Red Top papers are read by millions of people, including a lot of children, so any parent has to be happy that the stuff that you're printing is acceptable material for a young reader.

DOUBLING UP

On the massive stories, news editors will throw in everything they've got. Sometimes there might be at least fifteen staff reporters from one paper out in the field, as well as numerous agency reporters.

This was not a problem as every reporter would just be filing their own bits of stuff.

No, the biggest problems I've ever had with stories are when I've been working with just one other staff reporter.

Before you do anything else, you have *got to sort out who's in charge*.

It's like driving a car. If you have two people attempting to drive, you won't make 100 yards. One of you has to take control. On the ships and on the planes, the co-pilot will literally say, "I have control".

And as for two reporters working on the same story... I still come out in a cold sweat at the memory of the Wimbledon championships in the summer of 1996.

Most newspapers have one news reporter at Wimbledon to cover all the stuff that the sports hacks don't want to sully their hands with. But seeing as Wimbledon was such a big story that year, my mad-masters decided to send over TWO news reporters: young Billy who had just won his spurs, and another reporter whom we shall call Maggie.

Now Wimbledon was a great gig. I love watching tennis, and I love being out in the sun, drinking myself stupid and then charging it all on expenses.

It was going to be great!

There were a lot of news stories floating around that year, including the first female streaker at a men's final. The perfect *Sun* front page photo - tasteful, mind, with no pubic hair and just a hint of buttock.

My abiding memory, however, is of one wet afternoon. It's pouring with rain. It's been pouring with rain for ages. Nothing's going on - nothing whatsoever. I am becoming, as my grandmother would have said, "fusionless with drink".

And suddenly, from out of nowhere, Cliff Richard, Martina Navratilova and a gaggle of other female tennis stars appear in the Royal Box and start serenading the crowds on Centre Court.

Instantly, I know it's going to be the front page.

Sir Cliff leaves the Royal Box and has a cup of tea, and then an hour later, I'm scurrying after him to get his every last word on the story.

Things are getting a little bit tight now, time-wise, as it's gone 4pm. But we've still got an hour, easy.

Maggie is already back at the office, mindlessly rewriting the intro. Her chief concern, and I'm not kidding, was who the hell was going to get first byline.

Time marches on. Somehow or other, there's a role reversal and now it's me trying to write the Splash, with Maggie barking into my ear. Think backseat driving, only a lot more vexing.

And by now… it's gone 5pm and between the two of us, we have managed to write precisely fifteen sentences! For the first time in my life I am literally in a cold sweat. I can still remember the sound of Maggie barking in my ear, "Oh, not that bit there. Why don't you try it like this?"

It gets worse! The Press Association has filed! Two staff reporters have been beaten by those donkeys at PA!

My mobile rings. It is the deputy editor, Neil Wallis going absolutely mad and when you're on the receiving end of a proper tabloid bollocking, it would make your hair curl.

An hour later, long after the *Sun*'s subs had already started knocking the story together from the PA copy, I filed.

And that night I made a vow that if ever I worked on a story with another reporter, then I'd be happy to be the boss, and I'd be quite happy to be the gofer. But never, never again would I attempt actually to write a story with another reporter.

The years pass.

I've been in New York for two years with *The Sun*. I've worked for a year in the Westminster Lobby. And now, thrill of thrills, I'm being flown up to Scotland to cover Gordon Brown's marriage to Sarah - and who's being sent up with me so that we can reprise our phenomenal double-act but… Maggie.

This time I knew the drill. Before we'd even landed, I asked Maggie who was going to write the story. Eager as ever to snatch that first byline, Maggie said she'd just love to write the wretched thing. Not a problem! I duly scurried about, interviewed anyone I could find, and then like a proper gent gave Maggie all my quotes and left her to it.

Two hours later. It's way past 5pm. I'm having a cool beer at Edinburgh airport before catching the next flight back to London. I get a wailing call from the news desk: "Where's our copy?"

"Maggie's filing it," I said cheerily. "I gave her all my copy, all my quotes, everything."

"Well we haven't seen a dickybird," came the reply. "And anyway, what the hell are *you* doing?"

So, I got it in the neck for that one too.

And what I learned from my second (and last) experience working with

Maggie was that *I* should have taken control. *I* should have written the story. And I should have kept Maggie sweet by giving *her* first byline.

Be generous with bylines – particularly with rookie reporters who are just dying to get their names into the paper. When doubling up on stories, put your name last. Every paper will have a few reporters who are known as "byline bandits". Do not be tempted to join them. Sometimes, I'd just love to go the way of *The Economist* and ban all bylines. Only sometimes, mind.

MAKING IT WORK

Mad-masters *love* reporters who are capable of making a story work. They love to dream up a line - or even a headline - and then have the reporter come back three hours later and file a story that is precisely as per the orders that have been issued.

They are the Captain on board the 19th Century Frigate. They say, "Make it so", and the reporter makes it so.

This can require a lot of ingenuity on the part of a reporter. But just remember that if you *can't* deliver a particular line to one of the mad-masters, then you better have a damn good alternative. That's the way our game works. You give them their line and if you can't, you give them a better one.

Very often, the mad-masters will have thought up a headline long before the reporter has even started work on a story.

For instance… the singer Madonna had started dating a hunky guy called Carlos Leon. The Red Tops were keen to get stuck in…

Meanwhile at about the same time, one of the world's most ruthless assassins had just been arrested. His name was also Carlos, and he was quickly dubbed "Carlos The Jackal".

Now, bearing in mind the paper's predilection for puns, it was not long before one of the mad-masters dreamt up the perfect headline for the spread on Madonna's new lover: "Carlos The Tackle". Ha. Ha. Ha.

It was left to my redoubtable colleague in Los Angeles, Caroline Graham, to stand up this bonkers line. She soon found the requisite "friend" to confirm that Carlos was indeed hung like a donkey…

I'd been on a tragic story that had been rumbling on for well over a year. A young husband had died, and his dynamic widow, Diane Blood, had been traipsing in and out of the courts trying to get access to his sperm, that had been frozen prior to his death. Eventually, after a lot of setbacks, Diane won the case and as a special thank you to the press, every newspaper was going to be given a 15 minute exclusive interview with her.

Very nasty.

We don't mind press conferences.

But if you're all getting 15 minutes each, then I guess there's a small chance that you might end up with a really good exclusive line - and an absolutely huge chance that it will be somebody else who ends up with the exclusive.

Fortunately, the maddest of my mad-masters, Neil Wallis again, had come up with a line that he wished me to pursue. It was only mildly bonkers - for him.

The difficulty was that Diane Blood was a very, very bright woman. So getting her to say that her husband was up in heaven, admiring her good work and showering down his blessings... well, let's just say that I didn't much fancy it.

"So Diane," I said, tiptoeing round the matter in hand. "Do you think... do you think your husband... do you think there's a chance that he's in heaven?"

Diane doesn't quite know where I'm going with this one. "Well," she says. "I suppose so."

"And if he were in heaven, do you think that he might be, sort of, looking down at what's been going on here, and kind of watching from afar... "

Diane sniffs. "Well," she says again. "Possibly."

"Ahh, right," I said. "So if he's been looking down, watching this whole saga, then it's quite likely that he might be wishing you well. In a way, he might even be rooting for you... "

The penny drops. And Diane, being a sport, gave me precisely what I wanted. "Yes," she said as she all but rolled her eyes. "I think it is quite possible that my husband is now in heaven and wishing me every success... "

Goodnight Vienna!

The maddest of the mad-masters was happy.

When the mad-masters give you a line, you've sometimes got to be very creative about how you deliver it. But the one thing you do not want to be doing is returning to the office with a plaintive bleat that you couldn't make the story work. What will happen then is that the story will be given to a reporter who *will* make it work - and boy are you going to end up with egg on your face.

The Diane Blood story had a very sweet ending. In 1998, she had a baby boy, Liam, and three years later, Joel.

LIBEL PROBLEMS

Die Son newspaper had a big problem on their hands. This bawdy *Sun*-style paper, had been dragging Pinkie Pelser's name through the mud for over a year - and now she was finally out to get them.

Pinkie was a South African socialite who caused a brief flutter of interest in the UK papers when she had an affair with the husband of the Olympic runner, Zola Budd.

But although Pinkie may have sunk without trace in the UK, she was still big news in South Africa, as the tabloids ran lurid stories about lesbian affairs and bonking a barman behind his bar. One of her more memorable front page headlines was "Blowjob Pinkie". (It worked better in Afrikaans.)

By 2007, Pinkie had had it to the back teeth with being turned into this figure of fun, and she was coming out all guns blazing to sue the paper for libel.

And unfortunately, Pinkie had a pretty good case.

I, along with the ever urbane Charlie Bain, had been acting as consultants on *Die Son* for about a month. We'd been giving the troops lots of titbits about how things were done in London.

The editor, Ingo Capraro, called us into his office. "You've been telling us all about the Silver Tongue," he said. "Now put it into practice. Go up to Bloemfontein. See Pinkie Pelser. Get her to stop the libel suit."

Hmm.

Perhaps easier said than done.

We were flying out to Bloemfontein the next day and we still had no plan of action. It was not a conversation that I'd ever had before. "Please will you withdraw your libel action, it would make my boss really happy."

Well it might have worked. Just. But I wasn't banking on it.

It was when we were in Bloemfontein waiting to take Pinkie out for lunch that I had my revelation. Charlie loved it. Ingo was insanely excited. I just hoped that Pinkie was going to be similarly impressed.

When we saw her, she was striking in her ordinariness. We'd been expecting this man-eater, but in fact, Pinkie was this very shy blonde in her mid-thirties.

Both Charlie and I pinned back our ears and listened. She had quite a number of complaints; if it ever made it to court, she almost certainly had them on toast.

We listened some more.

And after an hour, when she was finally spent, I made my proposal.

She was misunderstood.

She was maligned.

Nobody *got* her.

It was time for the real Pinkie to stand up.

The next day, when Charlie and I returned to Cape Town, you can only imagine the looks of jaw-dropping amazement as I walked back into the newsroom. By my side was Pinkie - *Die Son*'s newest columnist. For the first month, she was going to have the extreme luxury of having her column ghosted by me.

The libel action was dropped and, for as long as it lasted, the Pinkie column was a spectacular success.

The more homework you can do before a meeting, the better. Every interviewee is going to have a weakness - some secret passion, perhaps; some odd hobby that has become their sole indulgence. These may seem like irrelevant details. But these are the things that are going to help you forge that connection.

* Pinkie was just 38 when she sadly died of an overdose in 2010.

PROSTITUTES

The Sun had some peculiar ways of toughening up its aspiring staff reporters - in particular, the mad-masters just loved sending the male reporters out to expose prostitutes.

And with me...

Well...

Perhaps it was because my mad-masters had decided that brothel exposés were the way to garner more readers.

Perhaps they were vicariously getting their rocks off.

But during one two-week period in 1995, I was sent to see fourteen prostitutes.

I was that wet-behind-the-ears reporter who "made his excuses and left".

Prostitute exposés are, I'm happy to say, going out of fashion. But there is still a huge fascination for stories about prostitutes. Not only is prostitution the oldest trade in the world, it's also one of the world's oldest stories – though these days our appetites are being sated by the likes of Belle De Jour and their daily blogs.

However, in the possible event that you are sent to expose a prostitute, here is the drill: tooled up with your tape recorder and possibly a video camera too, you visit a brothel, strike a deal, and then strip down to your boxers and ask for a massage.

The next half-hour is spent discreetly asking about their working life and any of the more bizarre things that may have happened to them. It's all very seedy, but fledgling hacks cannot really afford to be squeamish.

Two points. You must not, under any circumstances, have sex with the prostitute. It doesn't matter if they're stunning, and it certainly doesn't matter that you're "paying" for their services.

A friend on the *News of the World* learned about this the hard way. He had sex with the prostitute and then wrote up his exclusive, only to find that the brothel Madam had actual *video footage* of him having sex. This footage was with his news desk that very same day.

Most brothels have some form of video camera, firstly to protect the girls, and secondly so that the Madams can cash in if they're ever visited by a celebrity.

The other thing to remember is that, before returning home to your loved one, it's best to wash off all the baby-oil that's been rubbed into your back at £250 an hour.

After another of my daily brothel stories, I visited my girlfriend and I was absolutely reeking. How did I smell? I guess it would be fair to say that I - literally - smelt like a tart's boudoir.

There was a minor explosion when she realised just where I had been and just why, exactly, I was so fragrantly perfumed.

FIT FOR IT

A spring day in London fifteen years ago, and I had been tasked to follow a B-list celebrity back home with his young mistress.

He was a married radio presenter and she was, as I remember, a teenager. She may even have been still at school - but still old enough to know a good story when she saw one because she was the actual source for the tale.

It was all very cloak-and-dagger as I followed them back on the tube, watching from another carriage as the pair canoodled together. She was half his age, very pretty.

They got out at Hampstead station and immediately I could see that I had a big problem: they were the only people who'd got out at Hampstead station. Just as the doors were about to close, I followed them out. I was wearing standard reporter mufti of a blue suit, which is never great for a bit of covert surveillance.

I tailed them out of the platform. Obviously I couldn't get the lift up to street level, as it would be just the three of us in the lift together, which would well and truly blow my cover.

So instead I decided to run up the stairs. There were quite a lot of stairs - some 320. They were used so infrequently that the banisters were covered in black grime.

I started up the stairs. I think in my mind's eye I was still a stripling schoolboy who could run for ever. Three at a time, I took them - bounding up like a mountain goat.

After one minute, I was flagging. So I cut down to just two stairs at a time.

I'm gasping pretty badly.

One step at a time.

By now, I can't go another step and I'm stuck between the top and the bottom of Hampstead tube, hands on my knees, and this black spittle flicking from my lips.

Took me five minutes to get my breath back. Very, very slowly, I walked to the top of the tube by which time the birds had long flown.

That's about the time that I started to become a runner.

The truth is that every so often on a job, you've got to be able to run - run for a cab; run for an interview; run away from some screaming thug who wants to grind your tape recorder into your face. So, obviously it's going to help if you're fit. (And, quite apart from anything else, being a Red Top reporter is a lethal combination of the sedentary and the stressful; running is as good a way as any of staving off a heart attack.)

LEARNING TO DRIVE

Some reporters don't know how to drive - and for a while it's all just dandy for them as they're chauffeured around by fellow hacks or pliant photographers. At lunchtime, they can get as pissed as they please. At airports, they have none of the hassle of having to rent a car.

For some reason, hacks in Scotland are particularly susceptible to not learning to drive. A lot of places in Edinburgh and Glasgow are within biking distance and they just never seem to get round to it.

You can usually get by without a driving licence. But if you're a front-line reporter, you'll be much more versatile if you do have a licence. There will come a time when actually there *isn't* a photographer and there *isn't* a fellow hack to drive you round some far-flung country. And those are the times when, frankly, it'd be a damn sight easier if you'd got round to passing your driving test.

By the by. Surely one of the keys to staying fresh and invigorated is to have a new experience. Stretch yourself. Go outside your comfort zone. Passing your driving test seems to tick every box in the book.

When I was working in New York, I was flabbergasted to learn that my colleague on *The Times*, Tunku, had never passed his test.

I plotted out a magnificent game plan. It was going to be a regular weekly column in *The Times'* motoring section entitled, "Tunku's Crash Course in Driving". The premise was utterly brilliant: *The Times'* man in New York was going to learn to drive in the most frenetic city on earth.

His instructor would - obviously - be a very glamorous woman and week after week Tunku would be regaling his army of readers with rollicking tales of ramming taxis in Manhattan. There would be a large picture byline - perhaps with his glamorous instructor by his side. Next to the picture would be a number of World War II-style silhouettes, the better to record the number of "kills" he'd had along the way.

It was a total win-win situation. Tunku would learn to drive and would have all his lessons paid for. His mad-masters would get some sizzling, poignant and yet also ever so slightly hilarious copy from their man in New York.

After some considerable amount of badgering from me, Tunku made his pitch.

It was given the green-light!

An astonishing result.

Some fourteen years on, that *Times* column still remains unwritten; Tunku still remains incapable of driving even a dodgem.

ARE YOU EXPECTING??

Occasionally you will be sent off to stand up a story on a celeb getting engaged/pregnant.

THERE IS ONLY ONE WAY TO DO THIS.

Do not go up to your celeb and say, "Excuse me Miss Knightley are you pregnant?"

That would be an elementary blunder. All Keira will say is, "No I'm not pregnant, now kindly piss off while I sell my exclusive to *Hello!* magazine."

The correct way to ask any sort of celeb if they're pregnant/engaged is:

1. Present them with a big bunch of flowers. And 2. Say, "CONGRATULATIONS! What fantastic news!" (At which stage the celeb's face will fall into a beaming smile as she says, "Why thank you, how did you know?")

A SOCIAL FOOTING

Many reporters don't seem to be aware that, on a doorstep, they should be trying to get a relationship onto a social footing.

What this means in practice is that, wherever appropriate, you take round a little gift - exactly as if you were popping round for dinner.

There are many, many occasions when it can work brilliantly to take a present. The gifts we're talking about are wine, chocolates, flowers, or a cake (for birthdays). If there is anything remotely that your punter is celebrating, you should take them some APPROPRIATE present. Bereavements, obviously, are INAPPROPRIATE.

Use your brains and think about what they might need. Maybe they've just got back after a two week "holiday horror" - so what they might like is fresh bread, milk, butter, jam.

Obviously it's no skin off your nose what you buy - you claim it all back on expenses. But the gift is a fantastic one to bear in mind if a star is having a birthday, or celebrating an engagement, or pretty much anything at all. (Maybe chocolates if they've split with a lover; might work.)

The point about all these gifts is this: it gets the relationship immediately onto a SOCIAL FOOTING. And that's what you want. It blurs the edges. Most people expect hacks to be reptiles, and suddenly they have this nice, presentable person, who's even had the good manners to bring them a present. What you are playing on is people's innate courtesy. Most people respond in kind to good manners. They do not slam the door in your face. And they are unlikely to say, "Stuff your chocolates and go away."

AND OFF THE RECORD

Officials can get very, very nervous when they're called up by a Red Top reporter because they know that if they put a single foot wrong, then they could be out of a job.

This goes for anyone who works in the public sector. Doctors, police, council officials, you name it, they all tend to clam up just as soon as they find that they've got a tabloid hack on the other end of the line. "Call the press office!" they bleat. "No comment!" they say. Or, better yet, "I'm not authorised to discuss an individual case."

Yeah, yeah, yeah. It's all very wearing. And it doesn't seem to matter whether the council or the cops are in the right - they still prefer stonewalling to ever saying anything that might be of even the remotest use to a hack.

You may find, though, that the officials will open up once they've heard that magical phrase "off the record".

It means that whatever happens, they've covered their backs. They're not going to be named. They're not going to land themselves in *la merde*. They're not going to be out of a job. And they're not going to be losing their gold-plated pension.

But "off the record" has a number of different meanings. It is up to you to draw a definition that gives you as much latitude as possible.

For instance, how far can you go with the information that has been divulged in an "off-the-record" briefing? Can none of it be used in print? Or is it merely non-attributable? If it is non-attributable, can you still name the organisation?

All succulent little details which you will have to thrash out with your interviewee.

But "off-the-record" briefings can be a wonderful tool.

All *you* have to do is convince the official that you're 100 per cent trustworthy and that their name's never going to come out.

Next time you come across a tight-lipped official, try asking for a "totally off the record briefing", or "off the record background details"; a very useful phrase to have in your armoury.

BLUFFIN' IT

Ryan Giggs: superstar footballer; family man; all round good guy. I think we're all generally agreed on that.

But when it comes to dealing with Red Top newspapers, he's got all the intellect of a headless chicken.

Ryan had a very brief fling with a C-list model. Big deal. He's a multi-millionaire footballer, having affairs is what top footballers tend to do.

Yet because Ryan knew absolutely nothing about Red Top journalism, he ensured that the news of that affair - and his other dalliances - went right round the world. Of all the dozens of stars who've issued super-injunctions against the British Red Tops, it is Ryan who scored the most spectacular own goal. (And as for his "hot-shot" firm of lawyers, Schillings... Well I'm fully aware that they pride themselves on being the punchiest libel lawyers in the business, but I think that over this affair, the operative phrase for the firm would in fact be "Hot-Shit".)

What happened was that word had leaked to *The Sun* that Ryan had had a number of trysts with a one-time model, Imogen Thomas. Happens all the time. The news desk phones are constantly being called with pieces of unsubstantiated tittle-tattle.

Still, Ryan was enough of a star for a staff reporter to be sent to doorstep the model. She was in a total panic - but she did at least have the brains to call up the celebrity's Mr Fix-It, Max Clifford.

Now Max does actually know a thing or two about newspapers. He makes the patently obvious point that if *she* doesn't talk, and if *Ryan* doesn't talk, then no paper on earth would *dare* run with the story. Couldn't run the story. Not a chance.

Imogen calls up Ryan Giggs. "There's a *Sun* reporter standing on my doorstep!" she wails.

Ryan doesn't just hit the panic button - he hammers it. Schillings are called in, and Schillings issues a super-injunction to kill the story stone dead.

Except the story hasn't quite been killed. It's now got a pulse. By issuing the super-injunction, Schillings has actually breathed life into the story - only with a big, big difference. It's no longer just about a married footballer bedding a starlet. It's mutated into Frankenstein's monster. And what a monster! Before it even made it onto the front pages (of *every* paper, including the broadsheets), the story had already been tweeted by over 30,000 Twitter users. Along the way, it had also turned the British judiciary into a laughing stock.

Just *en passant* - I wonder just how much Ryan had to pay Schillings for their advice. They may know a whole lot about the law, but when it comes to the Red Tops, they haven't even made it to first base.

Standing up a story these days can be incredibly difficult. A few years ago, editors would be quite happy with a single anonymous source. They didn't even need to know who the source was. What was at stake was a reporter's reputation and if you served up a single source story, then you knew that you were putting your reputation on the line.

These days, stories tend to have to be double sourced, if not triple sourced.

It is, like old Hercule Poirot loved to say, "a little nightmare". How the hell can you double source a story when you've only got one source?

Well… We do have a few cards that we can play, and it's important to be aware of what they are.

The first is that just the very act of turning up on a person's doorstep can be absolutely petrifying - as Ryan Giggs' lover discovered. Most people have never met a Red Top hack before. They'll have heard about them. They'll have seen them on the TV. But they have never actually come across a Red Top hack in the flesh. And then suddenly, the door bell's ringing and they're opening the front door to find a journalist. And, seeing as most celebs are such total navel-gazers, their very first thought is that their story is going to be all over the front page of the next day's paper. They slam the door shut. They start hyperventilating. They're in such a panic that they're calling anyone they can think of to try and put a lid on the story.

Whereas… as anyone who's been in the trade for even a short time knows, the story is still a million miles from making it into the paper. Hacks are being sent on trawling missions all the time. The mad-masters are constantly sending out reporters to see what will happen.

I'm reminded of a little practical joke that Mark Twain once played on his friends. He sent them all a telegram, which read, "FLEE AT ONCE - ALL IS DISCOVERED" - and then stood by to watch as his friends raced for the hills, all of them quite certain that their guilty secret had been discovered.

Mark Twain's telegram is very similar to the arrival of a Red Top reporter on a punter's doorstep. Immediately they fear the worst.

So, on a doorstep, we are always doing our level best to be as charming as we know how. But it can also be helpful if you can lead the punters to believe that the story is going into the paper, regardless of whether they make a comment. This, as we know, is probably a total fabrication. But what you are playing on is the power of your paper. And when you turn up, all the poor old punter can see is these huge set of glinting tabloid teeth which are poised to start biting.

It is just a little bit of bluff. It seems like nothing at all. But don't forget that it is one of the most powerful cards in your hand.

I've seen bluffing taken to the most ingenious levels.

It was another ho-hum shagging story from the army. Can't remember what it was, probably a (female) General shagging a (male) Major, though it might equally have been a (female) Captain shagging a (male) Sergeant. Red Tops, as we know, are not very keen on reporting the details of gay love affairs; these are not considered to be wholesome family entertainment. But heterosexual affairs, particularly in the Forces, are standard Red Top fodder. Editors love them.

The problem with this particular story was that although the senior officer had been eased out of her job, nobody was talking. The General wasn't saying anything. The married Major certainly wasn't saying anything.

What to do next?

My colleague wrote up the story in his inimitable Red Top style and then had one of the subs turn it into what looked like the next day's front page, complete with a suitable punning headline. He gets a print-out.

Now ready for his bluff, he calls up the Ministry of Defence press office. The conversation went something like this:

"Oh hello, I'm terribly sorry to bother you. Just a matter of courtesy really. We're running a story tomorrow about the Randy General and her galloping Major, and not that we're expecting you to comment, but I'm merely giving you the opportunity to comment, if you so choose."

Now here was the killer-line. "Though actually... seeing as I've been dealing with you for so long... I shouldn't strictly be doing this, but what I could do is email over a copy of tomorrow's front page. Just so you can see what we're on about... Would that be helpful?"

He emails over the bogus front page.

What this did was it really focused the minds of the PRs in the MoD press office. They knew all about bluffs. But this wasn't a bluff. It was the real thing. There was tomorrow's front page - right in front of their eyes!

Ten minutes later, a call came through. "We're just preparing a statement."

And fifteen minutes after that, the MoD made its comment - to stand up the story in its entirety.

That is the power of the bluff. A lot of hacks aren't even aware of the enormous power that they have in their hands.

As in poker, even if you've got a busted flush, it can sometimes pay to pretend that you've got four aces. There are a lot of people out there who've never dealt with a Red Top reporter before. They can be very susceptible to a bluff.

AND DRINK

Alcohol, as I hope we all know, is a most excellent method of getting a punter to open up. Tried and tested.

Interviewee not talking? Just pour more beer down their throats.

Celebrity not feeling chatty? Just buy a bottle of vintage Krug - who could possibly resist?

Politician is giving a very lively imitation of a clam? Don't even ask for permission, just order a bottle of white, a bottle of red and follow it up with a double brandy.

Alcohol, of course, has to be used judiciously, and should be applied with our trusty staple, CHARM.

It works best over lunch or dinner and, just like when you're on a doorstep, you first have to work on getting a connection. Before you even touch upon the subject at hand, you have to spend at least two courses entertaining your new friend - by listening, by charming and by coming out with only the most entertaining and astonishing anecdotes that happen to be in your armoury. The workaday business side of things only ever comes at the end of the meal – preferably over a brandy. Doesn't matter who your dinner companion is – whether it's your boss or your client. Before you've got to the matter in hand, you've first got to forge a connection.

Pretty easy, eh? Well I can tell you there are MILLIONS of overpaid executives out there who like to cut to the chase before they've even touched the first course. No, No, NO!

And - of course - you've got to at least pretend that you're matching them drink for drink. Nobody likes to be drinking by themselves while their host is drinking water. And nobody likes to feel that you're getting them drunk on purpose so that they'll blab some loose indiscretion.

If you do get any titbits, go off to the lavatory and write them down in your little notebook. Don't do it at the table, it looks much too mercenary.

Afterwards, as ever, send a thank you note to your interviewee. Even if you've paid for the meal. That's what charmers do.

If you're going to run a story, and you want to turn your interviewee into a genuine contact, then run it by them first of all. They won't like it if the first they know of a story is when suddenly it's being splashed all over your paper. At London Zoo, there was a famous old lion called Arthur. A man had jumped into Arthur's den and after a partial mauling had been hauled out of the enclosure and taken off to hospital.

I was dispatched to interview the man.

My problem was that although I knew the name of the hospital, the Royal London in Whitechapel, I didn't know the man's identity.

Not to worry, I happened to know a couple of housemen who worked at the Royal London. And they knew the guy's name.

Obviously they wouldn't give me the name straight off. That would have been highly unethical for a pair of fresh-faced young doctors.

My plan, however, was to take the two lads and indeed their mates out drinking that night. I'd get them royally soused. And then - then! - they'd blab all.

Bloody students. They drank and they drank and they drank and after a gallon of beer, I was completely legless and the two fresh housemen were so full of beans they could have been about to start the night-time shift. Which they probably were, actually.

So... alcohol doesn't always work. But since it's only the oldest trick in the book, it's well worth giving it a shot.

One more thing. Maybe one day you will have that extreme luxury of being... A COLUMNIST. What a cushy job. Being paid a fortune to spout all your high-flying opinions, no research required. (Though a lot of people imagine that *anyone* can write a column. A fallacy - as we shall soon find out.)

If you're lucky enough to get a column, any sort of column, then it's very important to keep the editor sweet. She's the woman who's got her hands on the purse strings. She's the woman who can cut your column just like that - or who can extend your contract by another year. So, that being the case, it's important that you and the editor are not just colleagues. You should be mates.

Editors need to be properly schmoozed.

And this, as ever, means that, every so often, *you* take *them* out for a meal. Editors have seemingly unlimited expenses, and so are generally used to being treated like a cash cow.

Your treat. Just a small thing. But editors appreciate it. It shows that you're not just another sponger who's out for everything they can get. And it shows that you like the editor for themselves rather than because they just happen to be "the" mad-master.

The past master of this was the England cricketing legend Sir Ian Botham, who had a very lucrative column with the *Daily Mirror*.

One day, Sir Ian took the *Mirror*'s editor, Piers Morgan, out for lunch - and coming along for the ride was only the hottest cricketer in town, Freddie Flintoff. They sat down at their exclusive table and the wine was brought over. Quite a lot of wine. Just for starters, just to show Piers what sort of session he was in for, Sir Ian had ordered four MAGNUMS of claret.

That, my friend, is how to keep an editor sweet; that is how to get your contract renewed; and that, along with being poached by a rival, is another way of getting yourself a pay rise.

SCARE STORIES

You don't see so many scare stories in the Red Tops - probably because their readers have better things to do than fret about possible terminal illnesses that they won't be catching any time soon.

Scare stories usually work best in the mid-market papers, where the middle-class readers have got one hell of a lot to lose - their houses, their lives, their children, their pets, their pensions and let's not forget their shiny new cars. Amongst other things.

Britain's mid-market papers are brilliant at tapping into these middle-class fears, and at least once a month there'll be some splash about a new disease which is on the very verge of sweeping the UK, or some new terrorist cell that is hell-bent on wiping out the Home Counties.

Frankly, I think they're overdoing it. I mean it's possible to get a little agitated over, say, Bird Flu or Swine Flu, and for a little while you might actually believe that there *is* going to be a global plague. But, rather like the boy who cried wolf, you'd have thought that most readers would soon realise that we're not all about to die of cancer and that our pension funds are still bubbling.

But the Scare Story, used judiciously, is a useful thing for a Red Top editor to have in her arsenal. A good Scare Story will be about something that the bulk of the readers really care about. Not necessarily their health. But the price of football season tickets going through the roof... that might work. Scare stories about pets can do quite well.

People see the splash and they're so concerned that they buy the paper. That's the theory, anyway.

Ethics? This is a moot point.

If a Red Top splashes with a Scare Story, then for the rest of the day, millions of people are going to be agitating about that front page.

Now I'm not saying that these Scare Stories aren't entirely kosher. Doubtless the hacks have drummed up numerous medical experts to say that half the world's population is about to drop dead in its boots. It's just that... now how to put this politely?... despite all the huge front page warnings, none of the scares ever seem to happen.

What?? Stories flammed up just for the sake of a good splash headline? I am shocked, shocked to learn that such things could ever occur in a modern-day newsroom.

BURNING A CONTACT

As we know, it can take years to develop a really good contact. And unless your contact happens to be the Dalai Lama himself, then there is a very good chance that at some stage in their life, you may well have to write a negative story about your contact.

This is particularly so in politics, where even the best politicos in the business are occasionally going to mess things up.

Sometimes they're going to royally mess things up.

This is a big problem for a hack. You've spent years nurturing this contact, working them, taking them out for dinner, lunch and all the rest, and now you're suddenly going to throw a bucketful of cold water over them.

Fine. Burn away. Get your great exclusive and burn your beautiful contact. Just don't expect them to give you another story any time soon.

There are a number of ways of handling a story that's going to show your contact in a poor light. If it's a huge story that is going to be all over the papers then obviously you get somebody else to write it. See if you can get it toned down. Maybe write a personal piece to run alongside, your own close personal relationship with the star, to be written by "the journalist who knows them best".

If it's a story that you've got to write yourself, then there is a rather elegant little dance that has to be performed.

It goes like this:

You call up your contact, alert them to the story, and then pin back your ears as they recite their tale of woe.

Then. It's now your turn to say something. And what you say should go something like this: "Listen, I'd really love to kill this story. But, I don't know, it's just that it's already pencilled in as a spread... and if we don't run with it, then it's going to leave the most massive hole... and, I don't know... I just wondered... do you have any other story floating around that might just fill that space?"

This sort of horse-trading goes on every week on Fleet Street. In the worlds of showbiz, sport and politics, stories are being killed at birth all the time, and are instead being swapped for something that's a little bit more to the star's liking.

Occasionally, there comes a time when you weigh things up and you decide that a contact *is* ripe for burning. Sometimes happens.

All I can say is that you better make pretty damn sure your contact is totally out for the count. Their career has got to be so toast that the obituary is going to appear on the front page.

What you must remember is that stars are *desperate* for fame. They will do *anything* they can to perform a resurrection - and I mean pretty much anything.

How galling it will be for you when your ex-buddy is once again cock of the walk.

SPOILERS

I've never been quite sure how effective spoilers are at duping the readers - but what they are very good at is boosting office morale.

The aim of a spoiler is, pure and simple, to wreck a rival's exclusive. They'll usually have bought up a star, and will have done a lot of front page bragging to announce that it's they and they alone who have bagged that star.

Although spoilers are not as popular as they used to be, they can provide much merriment for the troops - showing that although your Red Top may have missed out on the world exclusive, you've still got one hell of a punch.

A spoiler normally takes up an entire front page and will be labelled "World Exclusive". To most casual readers, it will look just as inviting as the genuine story in the rival Red Top. The first few sentences will enticingly trumpet how your story, and your story alone, is the real deal.

Spoilers are painstakingly constructed from cuttings and from any interview that can be had from the star's extended family.

A lot of spoilers are largely about one editor pissing on another editor's parade, as if to say, "Stuff your exclusive - we'll just do one of our own."

And it's at its most acute between editors of papers within the same stable...

A Friday afternoon at *The Sun* and we're all gently coasting into the buffers. It's a sunny day outside. We dream of alcohol and missed kisses. With the early Friday deadlines, the paper has all but gone to bed.

Suddenly, the news desk comes ALIVE. Phones are being hit. Reporters are being dispatched all over the place. The paper's finest wordsmith, Mr John Kay, is called into action.

What sort of monstrous story could have awoken the giant?

Not much, actually.

It turns out that one of the news editors, my splendid friend Brandon Malinsky, has been off for a toilet break. There in his not-so-luxurious cubicle, Brandon has overheard two *News of the World* executives talking about an exclusive that's being readied for that Sunday's paper. Brandon doesn't hear much, but he learns just enough for the news desk to be able to piece the story together.

The mad-masters get very, very excited - not so much at the story, but at the prospect of being able to shaft their dear colleagues who are toiling away not 50 yards down the corridor.

The Sun was not able to interview the star of the story, who had already been spirited away to a secret location by a team of *News of the World* minders. But we did get the star's dad. He may not have said much, but he said more than enough to completely wreck their rival's exclusive. Job done.

TEAM BUILDING

Team building is best done over alcohol, though arduous physical activity can also work. Bizarrely, *The Sun* sent a crack team off on an Outward Bound course in the Lake District. I don't know what it did for the team, but we did run up the most colossal bar bill.

I, however, didn't have much time - or money - to play with. I'd just left *The Sun* to be the editor of a showbiz news agency, WENN. We were the Reuters of the Dustbin, picking up small pieces of showbiz tittle-tattle and sending them right round the world.

What I needed was a team building activity to show the hacks precisely how much fun we were going to have together.

I spent some time mulling over the problem.

The answer was an absolute gem: we went carol singing.

I hired a van and loaded it up with booze. Then, chauffeured by our one teetotal member of staff, we zigzagged our way across London singing carols.

Specifically, we were singing carols to the great and the good. We turned up at the homes of at least forty stars. We all got drunk as skunks. And we even got some pictures of Ewan McGregor joining in the revelry.

The next day, with only the very mildest of collective hangovers, the team had officially "bonded". We sold the story to the *News of the World* for a fortune.

Although hacks love to be treated to days out at the races and days out in the executive box, they will be just as invigorated if you come up with something fresh and original.

DRESSED FOR IT

On Fleet Street, there is an inverse law of clothing which states that the grubbier the newspaper, the smarter the reporters.

So - on papers like *The Sun*, the *Mirror* and *The Star*, suits are absolutely mandatory for the men. Women also have to look the part. I once saw a guy kicked out of the newsroom for wearing an orange shirt.

On papers like the *Guardian*, you'd often see achingly hip reporters wearing jeans and black leather jackets.

I realise that in most other countries round the world, things are much more casual. This is fine by me. But you want to bear a few things in mind. You cannot wear anything that is weird, wacky, or likely to cause offence. Tongue studs, bizarre shirts, crazy shoes, too much jewellery, novelty socks. Basically you cannot have anything that a punter - any punter - might find off-putting.

Dressing smartly opens more doors. Reporters are all about making an instant connection with people and if you've got something that they find offensive (tongue stud, eyebrow piercing), then you're twenty points down before you've even opened your mouth.

If you're dressed smartly, then it shows a certain amount of respect to the person you're interviewing. It also means that you'll be a lot more versatile for the many jobs that a reporter may have to do. It would be difficult to interview a senior politician or go to a funeral if you were in shorts and trainers.

Smart clothes can help you blend in. They show respect. And they create a good impression, which is vital for a reporter. Above all, you must not look remotely threatening. You look affable, smart, interested. Remember that it's much easier to dress down than it is to dress up.

Your hair is also important.

Now I could not give a damn whether a guy wants to have his hair long, or short, or shaved, or in braids, or in a ponytail, or even if he has the full top-knot and wants to look like a human pineapple.

But weird hairstyles are not a good idea for reporters. Reporters have to blend in and charm and not cause offence and there are a lot of people out there who think that guys with ponytails are hippies or layabouts.

If you're a guy with a ponytail, it's going to be tough work trying to form a connection with these slightly crustier people. Not that you can't form a connection with them - because you are, of course, a first-rate charmer. But it is nevertheless going to be more tricky to cast your magic-spell if, right from the first, they've started thinking, "Who is this foul hippie on my doorstep?"

I've got a friend in advertising. Let's call him Mark - because that's his name. I wonder if he'll ever read this book. [Hi Mark! How's it going?]

Mark is a guy in his late-40s, and he has a penchant for wearing black dinner jackets. If you live in Edinburgh, you've probably seen him around. He's the guy who picks up his kids wearing the tuxedo. Very snappy dresser.

And yet… Mark sports a long, thick, and slightly greying ponytail. Now this is fine when he's picking up the kids, or just mooching about Edinburgh.

But it just so happens that a key part of Mark's job is interviewing strangers. He goes along to firms and interviews dozens of members of staff, from the receptionists all the way up to the directors. He does all these interviews so that he can work out a firm's Unique Selling Point, and once he's got that, he can work out how to sell the product better.

Now, Mark is a charmer. But I have a big problem with that ponytail of his. A lot of directors, particularly those aged over 60, are not going to respect a middle-aged man who has a ponytail. This is going to be a problem if you are in the business of trying to charm people.

So if you're a reporter, by all means wear your nose-studs at the weekend orgies; and dye your hair red when you go on holiday; and wear lurid green beach-shirts on the way to the supermarket.

But when you're on the job... Well let's put it like this. It's tough enough as it is trying to get people to open up after they've just been involved in some deeply harrowing experience.

Why do you want to make life any more difficult for yourself?

IN THE NEWSROOM

The perfect reporter will, before she gets into the office every morning, have read all the newspapers and be fizzing with ideas for her news editor. Personally, I was always bloody hopeless at getting up in the morning. Before I got into work at 10am, I might have read one paper - the one I worked for - and listened to the radio, to have a vague idea what was going on. Only when I'd got into the office would I have a solo session with the newspapers, in which I'd probably read about eight papers in an hour. Not perfect, but it's what you've got to do. If you want to come up with story ideas or feature ideas, and if you want to improve your writing skills, then you've got to read all the papers going. Five papers a day, minimum.

You do also have to have your finger on the pulse. It is not acceptable for a news editor to call you up, send you on a story, and have you ask him, "Excuse me, what is that all about?" (No, this is one of many formal dances that you have to perform with your news editor. If he calls up and tells you that you've got to go and interview the first Martian from space, you do not say, "First Martian from space? I didn't know he was here?" The correct etiquette is that you wing it with the news editor, say you'll get right on to it, and as soon as he's off the phone, you call up a colleague to find what the hell he's on about.)

So, when you get in first thing in the morning, you want to at least be able to carry on the pretence that you're fully abreast with all the day's news. Another good thing is to listen to whatever radio station your readers like to listen to so that you know what's making them tick. You might even spot a fashion, or a trend that will run and run. This, as we well know, is newspaper gold. Editors love this stuff; they will pay a lot of money for the hack who can keep dreaming up new ideas.

TRACKING PEOPLE DOWN

Since the first syllable of recorded time, stars have had a standard fall back strategy for when the shit hits the fan - they quit the country and lie low. In some cases, they can hide away for YEARS. Four centuries back, the Earl of Oxford bowed to Elizabeth I and had the humiliation of farting right in front of the Queen. The mortified Earl sent himself into self-imposed exile for seven years. (When he finally arrived back at court, the Queen magnanimously told him: "My Lord I had forgot the fart.")

These days when a star lands themselves in the mire, they don't have to stay away quite so long. Normally it's about two weeks, as they sun themselves on some far-flung island, before returning home when the whole giddy mob of reporters and photographers has moved on to the next story.

An eminently sensible approach to a bad story. Keep your head down. Don't say anything - because every word that you *do* say will only fan the flames.

But on the other hand… well it's the task of a Red Top hack to track these scum-suckers down and give them a good grilling as they sun themselves on the Sandy Lane beach in Barbados.

Now the thing about tracking down these errant celebs is that it's never been simpler. And yet... it's a minefield.

Twenty years ago, about the only way you could track down a fugitive was to trawl for clues by knocking on the doors of their neighbours and their friends. One of my old colleagues used to have considerable success by snooping through the bins. Sometimes he'd find a catalogue or a confirmation letter. Just a thought.

Fifteen years ago, we came across a technique known as "Triangulation". Step One was to get your tame private investigator to pull the fugitive's phone bill, from which you would quickly learn their ten favourite numbers. Step Two was to then pull the phone bills of these ten favourite numbers, from which you would duly cull any new numbers that had recently been called. Up might crop a number at, say, the Sandy Lane in Barbados, and from then... turn up to the hotel. Get the pictures in the bag. Proceed to scare the pants off your runaway.

Today, thanks to "Pinging", it's never been easier to track down a celebrity. All you need is a star's mobile number and you can - if you know the right people - track them down to an actual grid reference on a map.

The problem, of course, is that all this high-tech stuff like "Pinging" and "Triangulation" is highly illegal. In the current political climate, if you were caught commissioning a private investigator to ping a star's phone, then you'd probably wind up in jail.

So... very, very dangerous waters. Me? I think you'd have to be MAD to start commissioning these private dicks to do your dirty work. Because even YEARS later, it can still come back to haunt you. Those email trails: they never go away.

This does of course mean that the mad-masters will be spitting blood at not being able to track down a rogue star. But who the hell cares about the mad-masters? They're always going to be ranting about one thing or another to the minions. That is their nature. But only a clown is pressured into doing something illegal. Besides - a class hack can produce more than enough scoops without having to do anything illegal.

We think. We ponder a problem. We use our brains. What an extraordinarily radical concept.

STARS IN BARS

As a Red Top hack, finger on the pulse, you'll occasionally spot a star in a pub or a restaurant. Sometimes a big name star - perhaps even an A-lister.

What do you do next? Go over and introduce yourself? Wow, I'll bet they'll be just thrilled to buttons to meet you - they've probably never met a real live journalist before.

Or do you sit there surreptitiously taking pictures of the star canoodling with his lover?

For my part, I'd call up the picture desk, and get them to send over a photographer. Then, at the very least, we'd have pictures of the star leaving the restaurant. I, meanwhile, would continue sipping my drink and observing how proceedings developed.

There are, however, other things you might like to try. They need some balls. But that's what we hacks have by the bucket-load.

The first is known as the Norman Wisdom Stumble. I've seen it done twice - with quite spectacular results.

Norman Wisdom was a diminutive British comic whose stock in trade was tripping himself up. I was in Buckingham Palace watching Norman get knighted by the Queen and he did a little fake trip both before *and* after he was dubbed.

The fake trip takes a bit of practice - say, ten minutes and you'll have mastered it. The way to do a fake trip is to catch your right toe behind your left heel. This has to be done at a normal walking pace. The next bit is pure acting. You stumble forward - and depending on how far you want to take it, you can even roll around the floor. It's your REACTION that is going to make the trip look realistic.

Once you've got the Norman Wisdom Stumble nailed, it's a cinch to put into practice when you spot a celebrity in a bar.

Firstly, make sure your partner has a camera to capture this beautiful moment on film. Then walk past where your celeb is having a drink. You will preferably be holding a glass or a tray of drinks. You stage your fake stumble. With luck, the star will either now be laughing or will be absolutely aghast. Catch them right, and they might help you up off the floor. If they've really taken a shine to you, they might even buy you a fresh drink.

There's one other ploy that can work with stars in restaurants. I'd never heard of it before. It is very unusual.

Jens Friis was a reporter in Bloemfontein who happened to be on holiday in Namibia. He was just having lunch in a restaurant and in walks one of the hottest stars of the moment, Leonardo DiCaprio, who was out filming on location.

The film-makers weren't taking any risks with their star, so Leonardo was accompanied by a very fit bodyguard.

Jens is wondering what to do next - all the usual things that a hack thinks of when they come across a star unawares. Should he go up to Leonardo... take a picture...

Jens went one better. He'd had some dodgy seafood and he fainted at the table.

An hour later, he came back round having been "brought back to life" by Leonardo's entire medical team. Instead of getting one blurred pic of Leo, he got the whole story: "Leonardo DiCaprio saved my life". Plus glorious pix. Outstanding!

OUR WEAK SUIT...

Twenty years ago, the strengths of a Red Top newspaper were very apparent. We broke world exclusives - and we could do them bigger, better and for much, much longer than any of those lickspittle journalists on the broadsheets, the radio stations or the TV networks.

But let's face it: this one great strength is now one of our biggest weaknesses. World exclusives are not remotely what they used to be. If you've got the biggest world exclusive going, it will be all over the internet and the radio stations before the first editions have even hit the streets.

By the time a Red Top is actually on sale in the shops, its news stories may well be over 15 hours old. On a fast-moving story, this is going to leave even the hardest hitting world exclusive stone-cold dead.

So you broke the story - well bully for you! The fact is that if you've got a monster of an exclusive, your readers will have heard all about it long before they've bought a copy of the paper.

This must all be damnably vexing for a Red Top editor - because although we're in the business of peddling news, all of our best stories are already out on the net as soon as we've gone to print.

Sports reporters, in particular, have got to be much more agile because with any big sporting contest, the fans will have already watched the event live. This means that Red Top sports hacks not only have to write up their match reports in 30 minutes flat, they've also got to come up with a new line to freshen up the story for the next day's papers.

It's the one massive weakness of a Red Top. Our news stories don't have nearly the impact that they once did. And we shouldn't pretend that they do. Instead, we should be concentrating on our strengths. And we have many of them.

OUR STRONG SUITS...

All those rinky-dink internet outlets like Twitter may be very good at disseminating the news but let's just see them have a crack at doing a picture. A big statement picture that will knock the reader right between the eyes.

Unlike the net, TV, or the radio, we can capture a moment in time. The only other people who can do this are the broadsheets - and most of them are still stuck with their high-blown principles of being "papers of record". There are a lot of pictures out there, which are of very great interest to the blue-collar workers and we should be making much, much more of them. I'm talking full front pages, full back pages and complete centre page spreads. Let's see Mr Twitter compete against something like that.

For big stories, I would love to see full wrap-around pictures on both front and back of the paper.

As for the headlines - well, guess what, these are another colossal asset to a Red Top paper. We need funnier headlines and, for preference, in billboard size fonts.

The Sun prides itself on its punning headlines, and they are legion. A brilliant splash headline can shift a lot of papers AND buoy up the entire newsroom for weeks.

A few of my favourites:

Elton John gets hitched to David Furnish - cue for *The Sun*'s mildly homophobic headline: "Elton Takes David Up The Aisle".

In the same vein, after George Michael crashed into a lorry: "George Michael Shunts Trucker Up Rear".

George notched up another cracker after being caught cottaging in a public toilet in Los Angeles: "Zip Me Up Before You Go Go".

The mass murderer Fred West hangs himself on New Year's Eve: "Happy Noose Year".

Cardinal Joseph Ratzinger is elected Pope: "From Hitler Youth to… Papa Ratzi".

A number of these punning headlines are too sophisticated to work outside the UK.

But even without puns, a headline can still have a lot of punch - from New York: "Headless Woman Found In Topless Bar".

The footballer Ronaldo out on a date with the millionaire bimbo Paris Hilton: "Ronaldo Has Night In Paris".

Britain in a spat with the head of the European Union, Jacques Delors: "UP YOURS DELORS".

Politician Paddy Ashdown is caught having a fling with his secretary - and the name that *The Sun* gave to him will stay with Paddy for the rest of his days: "It's Paddy Pantsdown".

COLUMNS

Columnists are one of the great strengths of a Red Top. Rather than merely reporting on yesterday's news, a columnist can give a riff on the stories of the day. This is what we are about. Let the radio stations and Twitter break their exclusives - we are going to be producing informed comment, analysis and wit. It's true that some of the best internet sites have their own commentators. But they're not going to be in the same league as a Red Top columnist who really has a handle on her readers.

For preference, I'd like to see a different type of columnist every day of the week so that come Friday's paper, we've had the whole smorgasbord: the trenchant political hack, the young mum, the sad single guy, the party-girl, and, say, the queen of the psychics. What we're aiming for is a little something for every reader. Just as we're striving for a good mix of stories within the paper, so we're looking for a good mix of columnists: the readers may not like them all, but will love at least one of them.

Or hate them.

If you've got an incendiary columnist who is really getting up the readers' noses, then that is a great result. Many columnists are judged by the size of their post bags - be it good letters or bad. The only thing that editors hate is a bland columnist who isn't in the least provocative.

The columns I like have a good sexy picture of the columnist up top, a lead story of around 400 words, and are surrounded by lots of little bit-size stories. These bite-size stories are important. Red Top readers find a long lead story very daunting, so they often start grazing round the outside. They dip into the little tiddlers first of all. These nuggets, which are often little more than a quip that's been overheard in the pub, act as the *hors d'oeuvres*, warming the reader up for the main course.

If there's a celebrity that the readers like to see in the paper, or a star that they're all raving about, then this is the sort of person that should be getting a weekly column. Big pictures. Puffs on the front page. Full spread on why they're so delighted to be writing for the paper.

Except - as I hope we all know - your star is not going to be writing a single word of their column. It takes years to be a hack. It takes even longer to be a columnist - so even in the unlikely event that a star is half-literate, they're most unlikely to be able to carry off a column. No, their column of course has to be written by a proper hack. The drill is that the hack spends a pleasant half an hour chatting on the phone to the paper's star columnist. All these ephemeral thoughts will then be succinctly boiled down into a full page of cattiness and bile.

There's also going to be a lot of talent *within* the paper. Why spend a fortune on a columnist, when there's bound to be plenty of young guns amongst the news reporters who're eager to give it a crack? The new mum who's still an adrenalin junkie; the football fan whose team is always losing; the young dad who's learning to cook. But remember that novice columnists need a lot of nurturing and a lot of guidance. It can take weeks for a columnist to hit her stride.

Illnesses and injuries may be harrowing and traumatic but they can make for wonderful, even inspirational, columns.

The journalist John Diamond was writing about his cancer almost until the day he died. On *The Times*, Melanie Reid was partially paralysed after a severe riding accident; her subsequent column was so heartbreaking and so perceptive that it regularly moved readers to tears.

These illnesses and injuries don't have to be first-person. Some columnists write superbly about the trials and pleasures of looking after disabled parents or handicapped children.

If a columnist writes well, then they can sparkle on any subject they turn their hand to. It will generally be "A wry take on… "

Good columnists could be trying a new job every week; or a new sport. They could be "The Queen of the Lunchtime Adventure".

If there are good writers on a paper, then they should be given every opportunity to show off their talents. Terrific writers should not just be stuck in the grunt-job of news reporting.

Now that I think of it, there is one other type of column that goes down a treat with the readers. I like to call it: Dirty Laundry.

The Dirty Laundry column is very simple. All you have to do is look back on various traumatic episodes of your life. Gaze at them. Gaze at them in the most minute detail and then dish it out to everyone and anyone who's rubbed you up the wrong way.

You are going to be hanging out all of your dirty old laundry in public and, very specifically, you are going to be naming names. You are going to be socking it to your spouse, your lovers, your parents, your teachers, your colleagues and even your snotty-nosed kids.

If you are going to put your life under the microscope, then there's not a person who can be spared - especially yourself. The only Dirty Laundry columns that work well are the ones where the columnist is capable of analysing and dissecting their own faults. If you're going to start pulling your punches just because it's *yourself* that's coming across as a bit of an arsehole, then don't even think about going in for "Dirty Laundry". They're awful! They're often shocking, you can't believe that a columnist is writing in this way about their own daughter. Often it's so ghastly that you're almost looking at the column through your fingertips. But boy is it readable! In general, Red Top readers can't get enough of your Dirty Laundry - but do be sure that you're happy for all of the very filthiest items to go on public display.

An example. Liz Jones is probably an absolute nightmare to live with, but she's also one of the best-paid columnists in Britain. Week in, week out, she was writing in the most toe-curling detail about her awful marriage. Eventually, even her boneheaded husband got in on the act and started dishing it right back in *another* column. That'd be Dirty Laundry Times Two. (Unfortunately for the husband, he wasn't much of a writer, and instead of sounding candid he just came across as a bit of a whiner.)

Another example. Even better. You'll like it, I know you will.

A few years ago in one of Britain's mid-market papers, there was an angsty column called "Daisy Dooley Does Divorce". It was a weekly column, about 600 words, and - unusually - there was no name attached to it. Daisy Dooley was just… Daisy Dooley. And if there are no names attached, then you can really give people a good chewing over; it's payback time!

The premise of Daisy Dooley was that she was a newly divorced woman who was trying to get her life back on track after a spectacularly ill-matched first marriage that had lasted just one year. There were tears, heartbreak and a liberal dollop of Daisy's home-spun wisdom.

As you can probably see, it's got all the makings of a *great* column. Perhaps even a book…

One character who would crop up periodically in the column was a guy called Jamie Prattlock. Even just going by the name, you can tell that Prattlock was one total tosser.

Prattlock was Daisy's dim ex-husband - "a puzzle-book addict pushing forty who thought that wacky clothes gave him a personality" - and although he was so totally out of her life, every so often, she'd give him a good kicking. The bastard probably had it coming. Besides, do you need a reason to loathe your ex?

Hmmm.

Daisy Dooley was indeed turned into a book, though thankfully the column has now been canned.

Daisy Dooley was written by my ex-wife.

Jamie Prattlock was a grotesque parody of myself.

TV AND SHOWBIZ

Red Top readers spend a lot of their time watching telly; I wouldn't be surprised if they were watching at least four hours of TV a day. The reason is pretty obvious. It's cheap entertainment, and Red Top readers don't really have the money to go out partying.

This all being the case, a Red Top should be hitting the readers' favourite programmes very, very hard. Particularly the soaps, where there is often a colossal gap in the market. The mid-markets and the broadsheets don't touch the soaps - so the Red Tops should be cleaning up. Ideally, a tabloid should have lots of daily soap titbits, as well as a weekly spread on all the goings-on in the soap operas. And the beauty of this column is that you get two bites of the cherry - first you get to write about the actors themselves; second, you get to write about what their soap characters are up to. It's bizarre. But that's what the readers like. So that's what you should be giving them.

All good Red Tops should have a daily TV listings guide, along with reviews of the best of the previous night's TV and tasters of the main shows that night. A lot of Saturday papers have the next week's listings in a giveaway booklet; these sell a lot of papers, particularly at Christmas.

Showbiz. Ah yes. I have a love-hate relationship with showbiz. It used to quite amuse me. Now I can't stomach it.

But then the very nature of "stardom" has changed in the last fourteen years or so - and it all stems, I think, from reality TV and the arrival of Big Brother.

Before Big Brother, a "star" had to do something of note to become famous - and this generally meant that they had some particular talent, whether it was kicking footballs, crooning songs or cooking up a family feast. Occasionally you'd got the odd rogue celebrity whose fame was based on them having bedded an A-lister. But the principles of stardom were still sound: you had a talent and, much more importantly, you had the hunger. And if you were really hungry enough, then you might just make it to the top table.

But with the advent of Big Brother, people were suddenly turning into superstars just because they'd been on the telly a lot. If you were on the TV every day for three months, then this alone was enough to send you into orbit. You could become a genuine stand-alone celebrity and the interviewers from *Hello!* and *OK!* would be queuing at your door, cheque books in hand.

That is why I don't have the stomach for showbiz any more. I mean it was bad enough when we were dealing with genuine celebrities. But the latest batch of reality TV stars? God give me strength.

Still, one should never let one's personal tastes detract from the mission in hand which is, of course, mass-market entertainment. And since the Red Top readers love nothing more than reading about the lives of the rich and newly-famous, then it is our duty to give them all the details.

It goes without saying that we're only gunning for the stars - whether C-list or A-list - who are of particular interest to the readers. If they're slobbering over Michelle Obama, then start regularly slapping Michelle's picture on the front page. If they're drooling for some talentless wannabe-celebrity, then I'm afraid that's what they have to have. This is the defining mantra of a Red Top. We're not preachy. We're not educational. We're giving the readers *exactly* what they want - and that is why we're counting our readerships by the million.

The beauty of celebrities is that we build them up and we build them up and then, before our very eyes, they self-implode. Don't know *why* so many celebrities seem to be hard-wired to self-destruct, but they are - and it is our special duty to record the ensuing meltdown in all its glory. Never forget that although Red Top readers love to read about stars on the up, it is their very great delight to read about a star gone bad.

HARDER AND LONGER

In South Africa's Kruger Park, a little boy had gone missing. He'd been missing for over a week, and his tearful parents had given him up for dead.

Then, after eight days, the boy appears out of the bush. He's tired, he's parched, but he's alive. It's a miracle!

South Africa's *Daily Sun* splashed with this genuine feel good story. And I should hope so too.

And yet the next day…

NOTHING!

This shows very poor news judgement. It's the sort of reaction of a Twitter user or a radio station. They have the one bite at a story, and then like a grazing cow they wander off to find something new.

But the point - the defining point - is that the Red Top readers will just be dying to know more about the Krueger Park kid. Give them the chance and they'd be talking about it for days. On this sort of story, you honestly couldn't do too much on how the boy managed to survive in the wild for eight days. Personally, I'd run it for a week, with all the lovely details about the boy's rehabilitation, plus interviews with any other kids who've survived out in the wild.

One of the huge strengths of a tabloid is that we can hit stories really hard. Unlike the ho-hum broadsheets, we can devote ten, twelve pages to a story. And we can carry on inventing new lines until the readers are satisfied and have had their fill. We can hit stories much harder than any other news outlet - and we can carry on hitting these stories for days on end, long after the radio journalists have given up and gone home. This is one of our biggest assets and we should be making much more use of it.

Over on *Sondag*, South Africa's Afrikaans Sunday paper, they'd had a huge response to a story on a killer who'd been imitating the TV hero, Dexter the serial killer.

Sondag had given the story a spread.

"They're gobbling it up!" said one of the mad-masters.

In my book then, if the readers are "gobbling" a story, then you should be giving them four, six, eight pages - and maybe more. And next week, you should be revisiting the story with a new line.

When the readers are gobbling, then you should be clearing out large swathes of the paper. No-one else can do this - least of all anyone who's babbling away on the internet. If they're hungry for a story, they'll buy whichever paper seems to have the best coverage. We should be squeezing the big stories until the pips squeak. Oh, and one more thing. By hitting stories harder, and for longer, you'll be freeing up the news desks and the reporters from the grind of hand-to-mouth news stories; rather than having to start afresh every day, the execs know that there will be at least a couple of stories which will run for the rest of the week.

If a story is worth milking then it's often worth dreaming up a new logo and perhaps a catchy slogan. Slap on the logo and a timeline whenever you have a fresh take on the tale.

FUN

Most news, by definition, tends to be bad news. Deaths and disasters are much more likely to lead the news bulletins than heartwarming stories about kids doing well at school - and the only time that a blue chip company is going to make it onto the front pages is when it goes bust or when the chief executive is caught out having an affair.

Many broadsheets have this rather serious po-faced view of the news. They're earnest hand-wringers who believe that we are always on the very verge of being swamped by disaster.

This is not how a Red Top should be. Unless there has been some epic tragedy, then the general tone of a Red Top should be fun. Light. Life may not be easy, but we can still have a laugh about it.

So we're still going to have our bits of gore and yuk. But I like to see a little playfulness in a Red Top, as opposed to the endless "woe-is-me" navel-gazing that goes on in the mid-markets.

It took me some time to notice, but after reading the mid-market *Mail on Sunday*, I always felt slightly depressed. I'd be left with this feeling that if things weren't bad now, they certainly soon would be.

Red Top papers should be creating an air of buoyancy - and that's particularly true when times are tough and, say, the whole banking system is on the brink of collapse. We're striving for a touch of the Dunkirk spirit. We like the general tone to be cheery. This is another reason why you can't have too much crime in a Red Top - because if all the news is gloom and horror, then it's difficult for the paper to have an upbeat tempo.

It may just be a light little twist on a story. But if it's fun, then that's an excellent reason for putting it into the paper.

A few years ago, I'd travelled up to Edinburgh for the weekend to meet up with a friend, Seb Hamilton. Seb was the news editor of *Scotland on Sunday*, and one night he asked his boss over for dinner. Her name was Margot Wilson - and she was, without question, the most beautiful editor I had *ever* seen. She originally made her name as Tony Hart's sidekick on *Hartbeat*; check her out on YouTube. She was a total fox!

Soon afterwards, Margot and I started dating, and within a few weeks I kicked London's dust from my heels and had moved up to Scotland.

I certainly wasn't in the business of telling Margot how to run her broadsheet - but occasionally, I might suggest a tabloid flick to a story...

We'd just had the 2001 General Election, and Tony Blair was back in power again with another thundering majority.

There was also one rather quirky piece of news in Scotland: after more than twenty years of the Tories being in the Scottish wilderness, a Conservative politician had at long last been elected to Westminster.

"That's a fun peg," I said to Margot. "What about a page on other rare species of animals that are being reintroduced to Scotland... "

Amazingly, she went for it. Probably the most "fun" that *Scotland on Sunday*'s readers had seen in years.

But these bits of fun should be absolutely standard fare in a Red Top. It might seem like "froth" - but froth is an essential part of the mix; it helps aerate all the heavy-duty news stories of the day. Without it, you're just going to end up with a block of stodge.

* What happened to Margot the editor? Well... since I've only been waiting over thirty years to write this line, I think that it might be the cue for a genuine drum roll, because... Reader, I married her!

AWARDS

The Darwin awards always provide a lot of pithy, amusing copy for the world's Red Tops.

The awards are named after Charles Darwin and are doled out each year to the person who has contrived to die in the most idiotic fashion - thereby helping the cause of human evolution by ridding the species of another numpty.

There's now not just a website with all the year's Darwin Award contenders, but also various books detailing the extraordinary ways in which the world's halfwits have killed themselves.

These awards have now gone into orbit. They have global recognition and are a hilarious annual event.

If a newspaper can come up with its own brand of award, then they can harness some of that power.

A number of papers have annual awards ceremonies. Readers get to hobnob with stars, and the newspaper is able to revisit great stories from the previous year with enough copy to fill a pull-out.

The most common awards are for some form of courage, with a number of categories ranging from stars to readers. Some Red Tops have awards for the police, education and mums and dads. Awards ceremonies are superb ways of raising a paper's profile.

In Scotland, they've got "The Spirit of Scotland" awards, celebrating all aspects of Scottish life. Better yet, the paper doesn't have to pay a thing, as all the costs are covered by the sponsors, Glenfiddich.

I was kicking the idea of awards around with some South African executives. We wanted to come up with some brand new award that might, with a following wind, become as powerful as the Darwin awards.

They came up with a beauty: the Moegoe awards.

In South Africa, a Moegoe is a nincompoop. And the winners of the new Moegoe awards are going to be the biggest morons of the year: the people who had done something utterly bonkers but who, by a miracle, had managed to survive. They'll be like the Darwin awards, but less macabre. And of course, there'll be several different categories for the Moegoe awards. The pop stars and the politicians will doubtless provide a very rich seam.

If you can invent an original award, then it can run for decades - and all to the greater glory of your paper. This is the future of Red Top journalism. We've moved way beyond merely reporting on the news; we're making it.

THE ELIGIBLES

There aren't many broadsheet journalists who could cut it as a hack, but my wife Margot would definitely be a useful addition to any Red Top. She is not as sly as most hacks I know. But is that necessarily a bad thing these days?

On *Scotland on Sunday*, Margot introduced a number of cool stunts - including "Scotland's Eligibles". A brilliant idea. Even years later, they're still running with it.

It's so very simple. Get a panel of five or six people and sit them down with several bottles of booze. The panel will then nominate 100 of the most "eligible" men and women in the country, 50 of each. Then: run a spread on all of your eligibles; throw these beauties a party; and finally, just make sure you've got enough photographers on hand to record all the fireworks.

This sort of thing makes for great copy. Red Top readers adore reading about beautiful women and rich men who are all "just desperate for love".

Like with the Moegoe Awards, we've got to be much more proactive about the news. We're no longer in a position to simply wait for the news to "happen" because when it does happen, it'll be picked up immediately by the radio stations and the Twitter feeds. Instead, we've moved onto another level altogether. The Twitter feeds can report all they want - but they'll be reporting about us and our babies.

Talking of which. A few years ago, *Company* magazine was running a spread on Britain's 50 Most Eligible Bachelors of the Year. They had a free billet for anyone from *The Sun*. I was nominated.

It all sounded like great fun. I spent the morning having my skin exfoliated and my nails manicured.

And then they explained that, for the photo they had in mind, I'd be naked but for a copy of *The Sun*.

One week later, my picture filled up an entire centre page spread. A none too flattering picture either. Perhaps a touch of lard. Enough said.

PESTER POWER

If you've ever been shopping with kids, you will know all about the enormous potency of Pester Power.

You've got perhaps 50 different things on your mind. There's all the things that you need from the shops; then you've got to remember to send that cheque to the accountants; and then there's also that vital email that's got to go out by tonight.

The kid on the other hand… The kid has only got one thing on his mind. He wants one very specific thing from the shop, whether it be a comic, a toy or a stick of fudge. And because it's just the one thing, he's going to keep hammering and hammering away…

So maybe you give in. Maybe you don't. But sometimes the screaming gets so bad, that it's just going to be a lot easier to let him have whatever it is that he wants…

Which brings us onto kids' stuff in the papers. Readers love getting their freebies from the newspapers, whether it's free pies, free maps, or free books. On the *Daily Express*, with its older readership, they always used to see their biggest sales when they were giving away free seeds.

Free toys are a great one. If a toy manufacturer like Lego will give you free toys for a week, then those kids are really going to start nagging their parents to buy the paper.

Personally, I'd like to see papers doing much more for the kids. We are, after all, purporting to be family newspapers.

Some broadsheets currently have a page or two of semi-educational stuff for the 10-15 age group.

I would prefer to see a weekly pull-out comic. *The Sunday Times* used to have a great kids' pull-out: "The Funday Times". Within a very short time, the Funday Times kids' club had over 100,000 signed-up members; that's a lot of pester power. (Bet you'll never guess who was the launch editor of The Funday Times. It was none other than my wife, Margot.)

I know today's kids have many different ways of entertaining themselves, most of them involving some sort of screen. But my gut feeling is that kids still love comics. Have kids really evolved so much that they no longer want to read anything that's printed on paper?

BOOKS

New books are not used nearly as much as they ought to be by the Red Tops. If there's any subject that is turning your readers on, then you should be PLUNDERING the latest releases.

It might be biographies of sports stars or pop stars; books on the Royals; or novels by their favourite authors.

These books can provide a lot of cheap, cheery copy, which - as ever - is going to provide a much-needed change of pace to the paper. At the top end, there are going to be the serialisations of the stars' biographies, but even little novellas can be hugely popular if they're serialised at 500 words a day.

Some editors even commission heavyweight authors to do them the equivalent of a Red Top soap opera. Get the readers hooked in the first week, and they can't give up.

But a lot of reporters forget that a new book can be a great one-off story that can be judiciously ripped off for next to nothing. All you need is a review copy from the publishers. If it's one of the readers' buzz-subjects, then they will lap it up.

If the book is fresh out, then that will provide the story with a timely news peg. But do not necessarily limit yourself to new books. There are plenty of old books out there which the Red Top readers would love - though they just haven't heard of them.

WAKING THE GIANT

A Red Top's readership is like a vast slumbering giant. It is huge and it spends most of its time fast asleep.

It is going to take one hell of a lot to wake that giant up.

But if - and that's a big if - you *can* wake the giant, then you will see how a story can become a monster.

Personally, I don't think Red Tops involve their readers nearly enough.

They ought to.

Many tabloids have over 5 million readers. That's an army of readers! And yet for all the use that the mad-masters make of these readers, most Red Tops might as well have the circulation of a local rag.

At the very lowest level, this starts with the "Come-on". It normally comes at the end of a perky or curious story, and reads something like this: "Come on readers! Have you got a pet that's even uglier than Harry the Hamster? If you think you've got the ugliest pet in Britain, then give us a call - and don't worry about the cost! We'll call you straight back!"

Come-ons are a great way of taking a quirky story on. They're essential if you want to start getting the readers involved. Most Red Top readers have all the news sense of a dead ferret - which means that if they're going to call you up with their stories, then they need a bit of chivvying. That is the purpose of the "Come-on".

Generally, come-ons are used for light, soft stories. But they're also useful for identifying people in pictures - say a star's new lover. I've occasionally seen them used to track down some celebrity on the run. "Have you seen the love-rat? Give us a call!"

You want to engage with your audience, make them feel like they're part of something. If they do, they'll keep coming back.

CAMPAIGNS

Red Tops are not just fun, family papers; we're also trying to show that we are the readers' champions.

This is the point of a campaign. We are trying to find a subject or a theme that is going to impassion and enflame the readers - and once we've found our campaign, we are going to do what we can to see if we can awaken the giant.

It will take some doing.

Red Top readerships aren't just asleep, they're hibernating, and it is going to take a long, long time to rouse them.

This means that if you're going to embark on a campaign, then you're going to need considerable commitment from the executives to make it work. There's no point in even considering a campaign unless a paper is prepared to keep plugging away for at least two months. If an editor gets bored with the project after a week, then there's no point in even starting. A week of campaigning is not going to raise even the slightest flicker of interest from the readers.

A campaign only starts to take off once the reporters and the mad-masters have got so monumentally *bored* with the subject in hand that they can't stomach another word of it. That's when a campaign is starting to bite. That is the sort of commitment that an editor must make towards a campaign - and if she doesn't commit, then the campaign will just be perceived as another of her odd-ball peccadilloes and will be hived off as quickly, and as painlessly, as possible.

Campaigns can work well on the back of a disaster, when a country has been engulfed by grief or fury. On these occasions, there is a lot of untapped emotion. Get it right and a newspaper campaign can become the entire focus for all this pent-up emotion - so much so, that you can even get the readers taking to the streets.

But right from the very start, you're going to have to be quite clear about the end goal. If there's no end goal, then the campaign will quickly start to drift. And - seeing as I can't repeat myself too often on this point, I might as well say it one more time. Campaigns need monumental commitment. These giant readerships are going to need a lot of poking before you can rouse them. But once they're awake, politicians will quail in the face of their awesome power.

EXIT STRATEGIES

About every other year or so, a Red Top reporter will come across a story which is so big that it's got the makings of a book.

I've had a couple of these stories - the Boston murder trial of the British nanny Louise Woodward that rumbled on for months.

And there was also Bill Clinton's fling with Monica Lewinsky. That lasted for about nine months.

But I never wrote the books. I'd lost most of my notes. I didn't have the time. And besides - I was haring after the next news story.

That's what hacks do. What do we care for some story that was big news a year ago? We prefer the hand-to-mouth existence of the next news story. Give me my next exclusive!

If you're going to do the book, then you want to plan ahead - you want to start keeping all the notes, emails and relevant pictures. It's all so much more difficult to do if, a year down the line, you're trying to play catch-up.

Piers Morgan completely appreciated this fact when he became the editor of both the *News of the World* and the *Mirror*. Editors are privy to a lot of nuclear-grade gossip, both within their trade and amongst the stars that they mix with. Not that any of this is printable… at least not immediately.

Right from the first, Piers had worked out his exit strategy. He knew that one day, he was going to get sacked. That's the way of the world for an editor. Doesn't matter how good they are. Doesn't matter how high their circulations. They all end up getting the heave-ho.

When Piers was in the editor's chair, he kept every single email and every single note. In the evenings, he would go back home and jot down the details of any of his spicier off-the-record conversations.

Then, when the inevitable happened and Piers was sacked from the *Mirror*, he set to work. There may have been a little embellishment, but Piers was intent on blowing practically every secret and every juicy titbit that he'd come across during his time on Fleet Street. Brilliant! What a way to leave the Red Tops!

As Piers realised, a book is a great exit strategy from the world of the Red Tops.

It might not seem possible, but after a few years of frontline reporting, many Red Top reporters are bored witless.

For me, it happened after I'd been on *The Sun* for about six years. I'd done New York, the Westminster Lobby and was now berthed on the Royal beat.

I'd just been to Buckingham Palace to cover my fifth investiture. I had seen Norman Wisdom get knighted and both Shirley Bassey and Julie Andrews turned into Dames. It was going to make a spread, and perhaps even a lovely picture byline.

An hour after the show, I was writing up my copy in a café in St James'. Sipping my coffee in the afternoon sun.

I was so bored. Monumentally bored. I didn't give a fig for Sir Norman and Dame Julie, and I didn't give much of a damn for *The Sun* either.

And when that happens, it's time to move on. There are not many things in life that are more debilitating than being in a job that bores you.

Jumping to another paper often works; or you can leave journalism altogether and sail into the scented seas of the PR world. That's going to take good contacts. But the top operators have planned their exit strategy long before they actually leave a Red Top. And I hope, in a very small way, that this little book has given you some of the tools of the trade to become just that: a top operator.

Wherever there is action and excitement in the country, there will be a gaggle of Red Top reporters who are right in the thick of it.

Except they won't be in the thick of it.

Red Top reporters are objective. In general, they are only ever reporting the actions and views of other people. They might be right there watching a front page story unfold, but they are never truly engaged.

The person who summed it up best was the reformed Tory Michael Portillo. Michael had several chances to lead the Conservative Party, but he never got his timing right. One way or another, he never landed the prize.

Didn't stop him trying though. Every time there was another Tory leadership ding-dong, there would be Michael doughtily entering the fray. He always ended up being completely mauled.

And one day, midway through another bruising leadership contest, one of the Westminster hacks went up to Michael and said to him: "Why Michael, why? You don't have to do it, you know. Why are you putting yourself through all this again, when in your heart of hearts you know it's going to be just hellish?"

And Michael just smiles – he smiles and he smiles, for he knows something that the hack does not.

Michael pats him on the back, and then he says, "Well... I'm on the pitch... and you're not."

The mad-masters may believe that they are movers and shakers, and that their big-hitting campaigns are helping to change the face of the planet. Well it's possible. But generally... we are the observers, sitting in our comfortable ringside seats as we watch all the action. But it's always other people's action that we're watching. We very rarely get involved.

And with me, I realised that I didn't just want to be reporting other people's fun. I wanted to be on the pitch.

Being a Red Top reporter is one of the most exhilarating jobs in the world. You've just got to know when to quit.

APPENDICES

The appendices detail three aspects of Red Top journalism that are a little too heavy-duty for the main text: writing, interviewing and negotiating.

Some tips, particularly on interviewing technique, have been repeated. I make no apologies for that. Interviewing is such a crucial part of our trade that I see no harm in running over some of the key points again.

There's also a section on writing for the Red Tops. Though it can take some years to master, I think - I hope - that I have produced a complete blueprint on how to write a Red Top story.

Lastly, I've touched on negotiating. Very few reporters have been taught a single thing about negotiating. It's probably costing them thousands of pounds every year. Minimum.

So although negotiating skills are only a small aspect of a hacks job, I thought I'd throw in a brief lesson. It is my small attempt to redress the balance of power behind the troops and the mad-masters; but then that is because I will always, at heart, be a front-line reporter.

APPENDIX 1

WRITING

There are still millions of people out there who believe that any moron can write a Red Top story. This shows a fundamental ignorance of what we are about. For although our style is short and punchy, it is deceptively simple.

Me? I had already been a journalist for six years before I started shifting on a Red Top. I knew all about the "Pyramid style" of story-writing, where all the juiciest news points come at the top of the story. But it *still* took me at least another year to understand how a Red Top story works. Years later, I drew up some notes for a young law student, Henry Meller. Henry was doing some work experience and did not have the faintest clue about how to write a news story. But he was bright and he was eager to learn. He nailed it within two days.

So here are Henry's Notes, now beefed up with the occasional explanatory note.

YOUR BASIC NEWS STORY

To begin: your first sentence has got to be a lusty kick aimed straight at your reader's crotch.

If you haven't got them there, they're onto the next page.

Before you do anything else - GET THE CUTTINGS. Makes it much easier to check the details and pad out your own news story. Once you have the cuts, you can start writing. In particular, if you're doing a follow-up, then you HAVE to get all that day's papers. There will be plenty of nuggets in them that will be great for your story.

Next - decide on the line of your story. If it's a fresh news story, then the line should be quite clear - the people dead in the car crash; the star who's pregnant. However, a lot of the time, your story is going to be about something already in the news.

Your line is going to be the fresh spin on the story. This will need thrashing out with the news editor. Occasionally you might come back from a story with a number of possible lines. Again, kick it around with the news editor. You cannot start writing the story unless you have a definite angle.

1. THE FIRST SENTENCE. You are going to start off with the subject of the story - the man, the woman, the dog, and you are going to describe that

man or that woman in one or two words. One adjective is allowed if your description does not have enough beef. Jealous husband. Cheeky milkman. Daft farmhand. Genius schoolboy. Just as the first sentence is important, the first word is very important. It's going to be the first word they see, it's going to be in capital letters, so make sure it's a good one.

2. We are now going to have the subject's name. This - obviously - has to be spelt right. We can cover up for a whole lot of cock-ups, but we cannot pull you out of the mire if the name is wrong. All names, even if they're John Smith or Tom Brown have to be checked, otherwise there is going to be a screaming tantrum from the news editor, and you will be kicked round the news room.

Occasionally, if the person is a nonentity, it's right to leave the name till the second par. But you still start the story in the same way - "A crazed sex-beast", "A depraved secretary", "A lusty cop".

3. So far we have just four words of the story, but you're off on the right footing. "Wacky chef John Smythe… " Occasionally you might be dealing with "Council bosses" or "Police chiefs" but the principle is the same - you start with the subject first. The main person. The star of the show.

4. Now, in around a dozen words, but not many more, you are going to say what the story is about - what the crazy chef has done that is suddenly making him so newsworthy. This is going to be THE LINE.

5. If you can, stick in the words "last night" or "yesterday" into the first twelve words. It injects much more pace into the intro. For instance "Genius schoolboy Alfie Jones was last night …"

6. If you're updating a story that's already been in the papers for a couple of days, then "told last night" or "revealed last night" are useful. These work brilliantly for splashes, especially if you've got an exclusive, when it would read, "Gun hero Alfie Jones exclusively told *The Sun* last night how… "

7. Finally. Here is the key to a tabloid story. If at all possible, use a dash. A dash is a brilliant way of pepping up a news story; it's a punch in the guts. "Lifeguard Jane Jones swam all the way across the Atlantic - with her hands tied behind her back."

If you can, use the dash. It will spice up even the blandest intros.

But do remember that dashes do not tend to work well in gritty stories like deaths or major crimes. That's because a dash has a slight edge of cheekiness and humour. On a murder story, a dash would generally not be appropriate.

8. You should now have your first par. It should be about seventeen words long, it should really just have the one news point, it should be punchy, and it should have introduced us to the hero of the story. More than one news point? Well sometimes you can get the second bit in after the dash. But if not, then have a word with the news editor, who will tell you what he wants the story to be. I love it when editors tell me what story they want - because it suddenly makes the story a lot easier to write.

If you're using the words "alleged", then that comes at the end of the paragraph. Usually, "it was alleged last night". If your source is "Friends", that also comes at the end.

9. Each sentence in a news story should be around twenty words or fewer - and each sentence will be a paragraph in its own right. Remember: No puns. If you dream up the most brilliant pun of your life, then laugh about it with your mates; possibly laugh about it with the news editor; but do not include it in a news story. If you're using an adjective, then it's got to carry its weight. Humour does not work in news stories - unless it's a funny story. Avoid flippancy. Try and avoid adverbs.

10. THE SECOND SENTENCE of your news story. You are now going to embellish the first par with a bit more detail - and again you're going to start off in the same way that we started the first par: With another couple of words to describe our hero. But use two different words that will give him a bit more flavour. So maybe in the first par we described his job, and in the second we might say that he's a dad-of-two. We are then going to give a bit more detail to the story.

So in our rip-roaring story about Jane Jones swimming the Atlantic with her hands tied behind her back, the next par might read, "Mum-of-two Jane only used her legs for the 5,000-mile swim, after realising she could more than DOUBLE the amount of cash she raised for charity."

Notice here the word "after". It's a very useful word, because it's a great link between the embellishment of the story and why she did it.

The word "after" also works well in the intro.

Notice also the way "double" is capped up. This can also be effective in getting the emphasis of your story right. But only use the capped-up word once in each story.

11. THIRD SENTENCE - we round off the whole story. This par we're going to start with our hero's name - either first name or second name, as appropriate, THEN THEIR AGE.

12. Ages now have to be standard for all news stories, except political ones.

If you are interviewing anyone for anything at all, there should be a standard set of facts that you have to have at your fingertips. These are their name, age, job, marital status, number of children, address and email address. You should also get at least two contact numbers as I mentioned before, one work, one mobile, so that you can call these people back to ask them more questions. There is nothing more irritating for a news editor than to have reporters say they can't get hold of the interviewees. The questions about age et cetera should become so pat that you ask them automatically without even thinking. BUT. Save them up for the end of an interview. Only mugs ask for these details at the beginning.

All these details will add flavour to your hero.

13. For the third par, we're trying to come up with a conclusion - a sort of "what the world said" - about the first two pars.

For instance, in our story about Jane the swimmer, the third par might read, "Jane, 25, is now heading off to the Olympics… " The third par should really be about THE RESULT of what your hero has done.

They very often open with the words, "Jane is now facing …"

14. Second and third pars often start with "And" or "But", and frequently contain the word "after". These three words are useful because they're little pointers to help you construct your story.

15. SENTENCE FOUR is usually a quote from our hero. Normally it's two pars of quotes, and starting off with maybe an adjective and then our subject - "Thrilled Jane said: " … "

16. In general we like quotes to start off with the name of the person, then a colon. Broadsheets like to do it all manner of other ways, but we like to keep things simple and obvious. Name first, then the word "said" then the colon, then the quote. It's bloody irritating to read a huge chunk of quotes but not know who's saying it.

17. After the quotes, we're now going to start telling the story right from the beginning. You want to be aware of what sort of show the story will get in the paper, so that you can decide how much detail to put in - but in general, if it's anything meaty, then you're going to put in every detail you can get, including the ages of the children, age and job of the spouse, you name it.

18. Now you're on your way, the story has to be interspersed with quotes, which help keep the thing alive. Too many quotes, or too much indirect reporting can kill a story. You're looking for a bit of balance. At some stage

you will have to include where the person is from. This usually comes a bit lower down. We don't want these details bogging down the start of the story. Readers also tend to lose interest if, early on, they discover that the hero doesn't live nearby.

19. All the juiciest facts have to come up the top of the story. Never save any little titbits for the end. The juicier the fact, the closer to the top it's got to be. News editors will have a tantrum if a nugget is buried down the bottom of a story. Me? I was bawled out in front of the entire news room for leaving a juicy nugget till the fifth par rather than the second.

20. HOWEVER. There are two things that you can save for the end of the story - and they can be very effective.

* The first is the blob. Suppose you've been writing a story about an elephant that's been put on a diet because it's so fat. During your extensive research, you may find that the world's fattest elephant was a 20-ton beast called Priscilla. That is the nugget that you save for the end. Just a blob on the end of the story, and you come up with your factoid. These factoids are just a bit of fun - designed to make the reader say, "Well I never knew that." It's any sort of weirdness or eccentricity that does not pertain to the story, but which is a bit interesting. If the story warrants it, and you've got half-a-dozen or more factoids, then you've gotten yourself a little break-out section. We like these. We like all things that break up your great screeds of copy. You've got to realise that your readers have TINY ATTENTION SPANS. A 1,000-word story is a monster for them. Sometimes they like to look at the blob or the break-out first, to see if it grabs their attention.

* The second is the come-on. Suppose you've done a story about a punter who's had his club-pass tattooed onto his skull. This might well be an appropriate time to ask the news editor if you should have a "come on" - as in, "Come on readers! Have you got anything wackier than a club-pass tattooed onto your cranium? If so, give us a call. Don't worry about the cost, we'll call you right back."

Come-ons are great. Sometimes they can last an entire week.

Those dull, dull papers, the broadsheets, will occasionally start stories with quotes or questions. I don't like this. This style can work in a feature but it doesn't work in a Red Top news story.

NEWS STORIES -
THE IDIOT'S GUIDE

After a couple of years of doling out Henry's Notes, I realised that they were a little too wordy for some hacks. So - if it's all a bit too much for you, and if you happen to have all the attention span of a gnat, then I have also boiled Henry's Notes down to Ten Simple Points.

1. Your first four words should be the star of the show - a description of your hero, plus their name. "Teacher John Smith" - or "Nobel Prize winner Bill Coles".

2. Then in around twelve words describe the whole story.

3. If possible include either the words "last night" or "yesterday". This will give the intro more pace.

4. If possible, use the dash. This also gives the intro punch.

5. The word "after" often works well in intros. First par should be about seventeen to twenty words long.

6. Par two (and indeed sentence two) should be about WHY the first thing happened. It may be a bit of history. It puts the first par in context. It starts the same way as the first par - with the hero. Though this time we might call him "dad-of-two", or "the jobless builder". It embellishes the first par.

7. By starting stories with our hero's name, you will give your first two pars more pace. More importantly, it helps you get the structure right. You're starting with the most important thing - the hero.

8. Par three is a sort of "What the world said" paragraph. It might be about the CONSEQUENCES of what's happened. Includes the words, "is now facing". Par three is generally about the RESULT of what happened.

9. Pars four and five are going to be THE DIRECT QUOTES. The style we like is the person's name, the word "said" and then a colon. THIS IS NOT DIFFICULT!

10. For the rest, you start the story from the beginning. ALL JUICY STUFF HAS TO BE CLOSE TO THE TOP. News stories should not have tasty little titbits down the bottom.

FOR A NEWS STORY THAT IS QUIRKY OR FUNNY ...

When you've got the hang of the basic story, you can move onto the drop-intro - the intro that leaves you hanging for two or three pars until the reader can understand what the hell the story is about. The US broadsheets love their drop-intros, especially on hard news stories, and IT DRIVES ME CRAZY. The drop-intro is all too often seen as a vehicle for a reporter to say, "Look at me and my fancy writing!"

If you are in the remotest doubt about an intro, stick with your basic news story style - it gets the job done.

But if you have set your heart on a drop-intro, then make sure that it is at least for an appropriate news story. It's got to be funny, light-hearted or quirky.

The world's worst newspaper, *The New York Times*, even decided on a drop-intro after several people had been murdered in the Empire State Building. Hard news stories need hard intros.

If you're going to use a drop-intro, do at least make sure that it piques the reader's interest. Not, "When Frank Johnson walked to work yesterday morning, he sniffed the daisies and saw that it was three degrees hotter than the previous day."

American journalists love this style of writing, and it is SHIT.

A drop-intro has to make the reader sit up and think "Wow, what the hell happens next?"

If it doesn't make your reader think that, then rewrite it. For instance, with our story about Jane, the woman who is swimming across the Atlantic with her hands tied behind her back, you could, if you really insisted, write it like this: "When mum Jane Jones swam the Atlantic, she wanted to make life just that little bit difficult for herself."

If the drop-intro does not entice you onto the second par, then you're stuffed.

The drop-intro should not be more than three pars long. By the fourth par, you MUST have explained what the story is about.

Even if you do have a drop-intro, then all the basic news values apply. Never, ever save good stuff for the end. The only juicy stuff that can come at the end is the factoid.

Some novices like to round off their news stories with a tasty quote. This is wrong - because if it's a tasty quote, then it should be up at the top.

However. If it's a feature story, then it may well be right…

One last thing: For any jokey story, always remember the ten songs. At the end of the story, we could have had ten songs - with PUNS in the title or the stars name. These are great for gags.

Puns are one of the easiest ways of injecting humour into the paper. But make sure they're fresh. Clichéd puns are plain cringeworthy.

FEATURE STORIES AND NEWS FEATURES

I love writing feature stories - because although there are certain rules, you've got much more room to do your own thing. What I especially like is that you can really spot who the decent writers are on the paper - and who are the also-rans. Suddenly you see that your esteemed executives, who know a whole heap of stuff about news, actually have a really leaden ear when it comes to writing.

There's no real blueprint for features - you're on your own, and this makes them much, much more daunting than a news story.

But the intro for both a feature story and a news feature (a sort of in-depth look at a news story) is quite different. A hard news style is not appropriate.

What you're trying to do with the intro is come up with one amazing fact or detail that sucks your reader into the story. This little detail should normally run over from three to six pars, and you've got to make sure it's a good one.

For instance, let's say that, three days after the event, you're doing a news feature on a shooting - twelve people shot dead, and a few injured. You've interviewed everyone you can, got hold of reams of notes, and you're wondering how the hell to start your 3,000-word story.

The question is: What is the quirkiest, weirdest, strangest detail that cropped up. Might have been that one of the injured men was saved by the ham sandwich that he had in his top pocket. (A nice detail, but inappropriate for a hard news intro.) It might be that the gunman was brought down with a brand new stun gun. It could be anything you like, so long as it's interesting and it's related to the main news story. But it's not the news story.

This little nugget is going to be your lure, your hook, with which you entice your reader into the story. If you can't think how to start your intro, then you could do worse than starting it with, "He", "She", or "It".

"He was the man who was earning 50 million a year, and with a mistress for every day of the week... "

"She was the actress who had slept with more Hollywood directors than... "

"It was called the City of Dreams - but perhaps a better name might have been "The City of Nightmares... "

If you look at experienced feature writers, they use these intros all the time.

If these openers aren't right, then try "As" or "When".

"As she laid out the breakfast, mum-of-three Jenny Jones looked out the window... "

"When he bent down to tie his shoelace, soldier Frank Smith didn't realise that he'd just saved his own life… "

What all these intros have in common is they take you INTO THE MIDDLE OF THE ACTION, without actually explaining what the story is about. That's all going to come later, when you can come up with all the nuts and bolts, the quirky details, (including age, job, number of children.) The job of the features intro and the news feature intro is to lure the reader into the story, but all the while keeping a few cards back for later. Features take a lot more practice than news stories, which is why they're much more satisfying to write. The only way to really learn how to do them is to see how the pros go about it.

After you've enticed your reader into your feature, the story MUST have a brief summary of what the hell the whole thing is about, before proceeding on normal lines. Just tell it from the beginning.

However. The ending of a feature is different. It doesn't just meander to a close - this one has to have a bit of a bite in the tail. It's the pay-off to the reader for staying with you over the last 3,000 words.

This pay-off is often done with a juicy quote, which can be a wry summary of the whole thing. Or it can go back to the beginning.

Numerous features end where they started - bringing the wheel full circle. If you haven't got a decent quote, then see if you can finish the thing where you started.

MONSTER SPLASHES

Once or twice a year, there will be a Monster Splash - a news story for which the mad-masters are going to clear most of the paper.

For these major world events, your bog-standard splash intro is going to need some beefing up. Just writing, "The world was in mourning last night after… " is not really going to cut it.

These stories require not just considerable skill, but also call for a quality that you won't often find in a Red Top hack. They need POETRY. The reporter almost has to capture the emotion of the story and weigh up the whole drama of what has occurred.

You'll be not so much reporting the facts, as diving into the actual emotions that will be welling up in the readers' hearts.

After Princess Diana's death in 1997, the *Mirror*'s poetry managed to capture some of that emotion: "For seventeen years Diana was part of our lives. Now where she was there is a void.

"We will miss the brightness, gaiety and glamour she brought to us.

"We will miss the controversy she created and the fascination she held for untold millions.

"We will miss the love she showed to the sick, poor and desperate around the world."

On the flip side, I give you the splash intro in *The Scotsman* the day after 9/11. It is so awful that it has gone down in Fleet Street history: "We have seen this sort of thing before, in King Kong, in Godzilla, in Independence Day. But this was not the popcorn logic of Hollywood. This horror was real."

This is a shockingly bad intro for a number of reasons. It is crass and it is flippant, and it is staggeringly inappropriate for a disaster that's just left 3,000 dead.

APPENDIX 2

INTERVIEWING

As I may have pointed out, charm is a much underrated skill. But it is a skill, not a talent and it has to be practised. It is also much more effective face to face, so if you have the option, always see the punters in person. You can do a lot of work on the phone, but going to the house will work much better.

First things first, if you're being sent on a doorstep, then try and do as much homework as you can. If you've time, then get the cuts. Think about the killer questions; get some sort of steer from the news editor about what sort of line is being pitched in conference.

More often than not, however, there is no editorial line, no cuts, and you've just been thrown straight into the story. "Go and interview Mrs McDonald," the boss says. "She'd just got married and was on the first night of their honeymoon. Her husband had just stepped outside the caravan and was killed by a bolt of lightning."

It's a great story - and the key is whether you're going to be able to get Mrs McDonald to talk. This is what the whole business of our craft revolves around: Can you get the person to open up?

It is a skill, and no matter what your career-path, it will stand you in good stead for the rest of your life. And it doesn't even make much odds if every newspaper in the world goes to the wall - because the reporters are always going to be fine and dandy. They are the front-line troops and their services will always be in demand because, no matter what happens in this world, no matter if every jot of news comes over the web, we are always going to need the reporters, the hacks, who are going to dig up the stories in the first place.

This is how you're going to dig up that diamond of a story.

1. You're looking smart. That should be a given. Nose-studs and orange shirts have all been removed. Nothing too flash either.

2. On big breaking stories, you have to get there as quickly as possible. First reporter in can usually clean up. If you're the second reporter arriving on a story, and there's already someone in there oozing charm from every pore, then it's much more difficult. So get there fast. If you're going with a photographer, he drives, you direct and above all you're on the phone. You're finding out as much as you can about the story before you arrive. Thanks to your phone calls, you know that Mrs McDonald's name is Sheila, her dead husband was Andy, and that they were engaged for a year before their wedding.

3. You've arrived at Mrs McDonald's house. If you have time, do some reconnaissance. Drive past, check out the drive, the garden. Are there any other hacks already there? Maybe the mob's already arrived? What's the garden like? Are they keen gardeners? Do they have children? Do they have pets? Size up the value of the property and note it down - it all adds for nice detail in the copy if you can describe their home as a four-bed bungalow, or a two-bed semi. We like these sort of details.

4. Tape recorders. Some reporters keep their tape-recorders in their top pockets, the better to record every word that is said. Some don't. This is up to you. It is definitely sneaky. It may even be illegal. And if the tape recorder is discovered then there will be one hell of a row.

But on the other hand, you may not get more than a minute with Sheila McDonald. If you've got every word on tape, you'll have enough for a page lead.

5. It might seem now that it's just a simple matter of knocking on the door, asking if you can chat, and then seeing whether she's going to slam the door in your face. This is facile. There are many, many things that you now can do to worm your way into the house. But first…

6. Keep the photographer under control. No matter how experienced your photographer, it is the reporter who is ALWAYS in charge of the mission. It is the reporter who does the chat, and it is going to be the reporter who gets the team through the front door.

7. One last thing before you go in. Would it be at all appropriate to bring a gift? In Mrs McDonald's case - a bereavement - obviously not.

But there are many, many occasions when it can work brilliantly to take a gift. The gifts we're talking about are wine, chocolates, flowers, or a cake (for birthdays). The point about all these gifts is this: It gets the relationship immediately onto *a social footing*.

8. Hold people's gaze much, much longer than you have been doing in the past. Sunglasses must come off - ALWAYS.

THE DETAIL OF
THE DOORSTEP

We are still on the lightning strike story of poor Mrs McDonald whose husband was killed by lightning on the first night of their honeymoon.

A. Going up the garden path. If the gate's closed, close it behind you. Leave everything how it was - because they may well be watching you. Guys - if you want to make sure your fly is done up then do it beforehand. Princess Diana's mum said that every male hack who visited her used to do up their flies as they went up the path. Creates a poor impression. Slightly skanky. And we are all about creating GOOD, CARING, CONSIDERATE first impressions.

B. You knock, ring on the bell. If your photographer cannot keep his mouth shut, then you do not want him anywhere near you at this critical stage. Leave him in the car, whatever, but do not have him queering your pitch.

C. After you've knocked, take at least two or three steps back so that when McDonald comes to the door, she's not got this monster right on the doorstep - she's got a very nice, well-dressed man or woman standing diffidently on the path. Do not have a notepad in your hand. Many people recoil at the sight of a notepad.

D. The opening line - this is vital. You are looking to show some sort of empathy with the woman, and you can do a lot worse than this standard opener, "I'm very sorry to bother you at a time like this... "

E. Usually it won't be Mrs McDonald who comes to the door, it'll be somebody else - they'll say, "what do you want?"

F. You now have to get past the gatekeeper. You repeat that YOU'RE VERY SORRY TO BOTHER THEM. This should be so well honed that it's a mantra. Then you have to identify yourself - quickly - just name and the name of your paper. Then we get on to the matter in hand. "I wondered if it would be possible just to have the briefest of words with Sheila." Use her first name. This is important; immediately puts you on a cosy footing.

G. The gatekeeper says she'll go off to find Sheila, comes back a minute later, and tells you to sod off. You, however, do not sod off. You are not going to leave until the door is physically slammed in your face. (At which stage you leave and return an hour later.)

H. What you do is: GO BIG ON THE EMPATHY. Something like, "I appreciate that it must be such a terrible time for you all. It must be so difficult for Sheila now." (You ask a question which is going to get the answer Yes.)

I. Continue down this line. The idea is that you are going to keep talking and talking and talking. There is not going to be a lull. The gatekeeper might just be saying, "yes", "yes", but you're going to fill in the gaps. It goes without saying that if she wants to talk, then you SHUT YOUR MOUTH. If she wants to tell you the moon is made of cheese, you put on your most interested face, and ask your most interested questions.

If she's never seen a reporter before, then she'll be unlikely to slam the door in your face. What you are looking for is SOME SORT OF CONNECTION. The gatekeeper is going to be very wary - so don't talk about the subject in hand at all.

THIS IS THE MOST BASIC ERROR THAT REPORTERS MAKE. They go in for the kill. What you should be doing is trying to get a connection.

J. After a minute or so, you are going to move off from the awful trauma, and you're going to start talking about the garden; or the lovely car; or even the weather. Better yet, a dog is going to poke its nose round the door and you're going to make a fuss of it, pat it till it's rolling on the ground. Even better, there might be a kid. This you are going to dote on as if it were your own first-born. Even if the kid looks like a troll, you are going to say, "Isn't he gorgeous. What a lovely baby." No parent can get enough of how lovely their kid is - and pet-owners are also not averse to hearing how lovely their pooch is, and how you've got one just like it. Whatever happens, you're going to keep on talking about whatever comes into your head, so that the gatekeeper sees that you're human. Kids and pets are great - especially if you have one yourself.

K. Now, after about five minutes, or after a suitable connection has been made, you can then say, "Well I'll be off then, thanks so much for taking the time to talk to me, and what a lovely dog you have." Then you ask again, "There isn't just a chance that I could have a brief word with Sheila... it wouldn't be more than a minute. I realise this is an awful time for her." Then the killer line: "WE WERE REALLY JUST LOOKING FOR ANY SORT OF TRIBUTE ABOUT HER HUSBAND. I can see he was a wonderful man/dad, and I wondered if she'd like to share that with our readers."

L. Let's hope that at this stage you're in. If not, you just keep talking,

talking, trying to get any connection at all. Do not get too close. But you're not going to leave until that door is shut. If she asks your name, give your full name, but then say, "Just call me Bill/Jane." YOU WANT THEM TO CALL YOU BY YOUR FIRST NAME. Remember to be wary about calling older people by their first names - this would be a blunder. Many people in their sixties like to keep things more formal.

M. Once you're in, you're in. If you haven't done so already, now is the time to BUILD ON THAT CONNECTION. Maybe they've let you straight in. Now is the time that you have to CHARM, CHARM, CHARM. Could be the picture on the wall. The golf clubs in the passage. The kids' toys. The astonishing antique sideboard in the corner. It does not matter. You need to have that connection outside the main story. This might seem wrong - because all you want to talk about is the story. But in order to get them to open up, you have to first have the connection. The interviewee has got to like you - and this could be because you patted their dog, or liked their roses, or even that you're a golfer. Better yet, you've got kids just like they do. Kid and pet anecdotes are BRILLIANT for getting that connection.

If the worst comes to worst, and you can think of absolutely nothing to say, then revert to the weather. It'll keep you going for a minute, until you can think of some better topic of conversation. Failing that, you could even praise the house. "What a lovely house... what wonderful light... "

N. You're ushered into Sheila's presence. You repeat what you've said before to the gatekeeper, "I'm so very sorry to bother you, it must be such an awful time for you..."

O. The woman may just dumbly nod her head, and what you are going to do now is EMPATHISE. You are going to say anything at all that comes into your head that shows you feel her pain. Do not let there be a long gap, as you think what the hell to say. Some real pros get down on their knees, and get all touchy-feely, but I've never had the stomach for that.

P. If you can, sit down with them. Build on that connection.

Q. I cannot emphasise enough that the key to getting people's stories, is to first get the connection. If you don't get it, then you'll be out on your ear in under 3 minutes. But if people feel they have some sort of bond with you, then they're going to be more likely to chat. And, crucially, you're less likely to be given the boot when a rival reporter comes to the door. When you've got the connection down pat, only then can you move on to the delicate matter of the story. Start slow - ask for any sort of tribute that they'd like to make to their dead husband. Only when they're properly revved up can you start asking for the gory details.

R. If you are offered any drink at all - from tea to crème de menthe - you accept it. You don't have to drink it. Take your coat off. You are settling yourself down. You're in for the duration.

S. Once you have your main person talking, be wary about butting in too much. Let them tell their story, and leave the detail questions for later. But do not leave these details out. At the end, after the whole thing is done and dusted, you have to say these magic words: "I wondered if I could just check the correct spelling of your names; and do you mind if I ask how old you are; and how old is Andy; and what was his job; and could I just check how many children you have... "et cetera.

T. There is a correct way to get out your notepad. Only once the interviewee is fully in flow do you say, "Do you mind if I take a note of this... " while at the same time getting the pad out. Do not leave it too late, because otherwise all these beautiful pearls are going to be lost. You've worked hard to get this far, don't miss out now.

U. Later on still, you may bring up the matter of your photographer. Do not spoil the flow by asking about pics when you still haven't got the whole story. If the photographer is with you, then he should be following your lead. A few photographers can do the charm thing... but most should know that their sole job is TO KEEP THEIR MOUTHS SHUT. HOWEVER - a photographer can be very useful at keeping the opposition out. If you're being interrupted by rival reporters at the front door, leave it to the photographer to keep them out. Standard procedure is to tell the interviewee not even to let the opposition into the house. DO NOT OPEN THE DOOR - otherwise things will get tense.

V. If you're on a story where rival reporters are likely to mess things up, then get your stars out of the house as quickly as possible.

W. Finally - you've got the whole story, you've got every detail you need, you've got all the contact numbers you want. Now it's time for the pictures. A lot of good pictures can be found on Facebook.
If you can, take the albums - this makes it much more difficult for the opposition when they turn up five minutes later. It's now that you give your last question. Let's say there's a question that has to be asked that they might well take offence at. You ask this question last of all, when their guard's down. Worst comes to worst, you may get thrown out - but at least you've already got the whole story in your notebook. The last killer question works especially

well with celebrities. The tastiest celeb quotes often occur when the reporter is leaving.

X. Off you go and file your copy the moment you're out the door. The etiquette is that FIRST CALL IS TO THE NEWS EDITOR. He wants to know what the hell you've been doing this past hour; give him an outline of the story. Then file - and file quickly.

Y. When the splash appears the next day, you might give yourself a little pat on the back before moving onto the next story. The professionals will go back to the interviewee in person - not only to return the photo album, but to check that they're okay and were happy with the story. The reason why the pros keep the interviewees sweet is so that they'll get any follow-ups. Such as... This very story about the lightning strike actually occurred. I was lucky enough to be the first reporter in. It had the most astonishing follow-up. It turned out that the very day that the woman's husband was killed, she'd conceived their first child. Guess who had the splash nine months later.

Z. Lastly and most importantly, back at the office you're going to transcribe all your contact's numbers into your contacts-book, so that, five years down the line and you're looking to do a feature on lightning strikes, you've got all her details at the touch of a button.

APPENDIX 3

NEGOTIATING

Reporters know next to nothing about negotiating. Once every three years they go into the editor's office to negotiate a pay rise and they end up getting absolutely shafted. That's because most editors - unlike the reporters - have a deal of experience in negotiating. They've probably been on a business course. They will be negotiating new contracts every day of the week.

So, in a very small attempt to redress the balance, I drew up two negotiating exercises. They're little games that call for some role-playing. But the results are utterly compelling. You will learn more about negotiating from playing these games than you will learn from reading any book.

In order for the games to work best, both negotiators - obviously - have to be kept in the dark about the other player's position. Better still, you've got a number of people pairing off to play the game at the same time - so that at the end, they can all compare notes. That way, you'll end up with a winner - and you'll also end up with a loser who, we hope, will have learned the lesson of a lifetime. (Are you hearing me, Inge Liebenberg?)

So - go get someone else to organise the game - AND NO PEEKING!

GAME 1 - THE JOB

NOTES FOR THE BOSS

You are an editor in chief at Hack.Corp - you've got hundreds of hacks, an army of them, at your disposal and a lot of money too. Your name is going to be: THE BOSS.

You're looking to launch a new paper, and there is one very specific person to run this paper. We shall call this person: TOP GUN!

Now, realistically, Top Gun is the only person who can run this paper. He's got a lot of experience. He's associate editor of a very similar title and now you're looking to move him up to edit this new paper. You could go off to some other firm, poach somebody else - but really, you've only got one person in mind for the job. That is Top Gun.

You've also got a lot of money for Top Gun. Top Gun is currently on £50,000 a year. You are prepared to go to anything up to £250,000 a year. You can also offer him a golden handshake - that's a lump sum to kick off with, just as a thank you for signing on. You'll be happy to go up to £75,000. But it goes without saying that you'd like to get Top Gun as cheap as you can. This will mean more money for the paper and more bonuses. All the usual stuff.

There are some other things you should bear in mind. Because of various bits of office politics, Top Gun is going to be running the paper, but he's only going to be the deputy. The editor is going to be a sort of editor across two titles. It's unusual but that's office politics for you. You'd much prefer it - and it would be much easier for you - if Top Gun would accept just being the deputy. But if Top Gun gets tough, then you will be prepared to concede this point.

Top Gun may also want a company car. Company cars are going to set the firm back about £20,000 a year. See what you can get away with.

Top Gun may also want a secretary. The secretary will probably be £20,000. Again, not essential. You have bargaining power on this one.

The main thing is you've got to get your man. Other newspaper groups have been sniffing around Top Gun, and might well pinch him to set up a different title.

GOOD LUCK!

GAME 1 - THE JOB

You are an associate editor for one of the Tabloid titles at Hack.Corp. That means you're about number three or four on the paper. But you're very good at your job - the hack who's driving the whole show. Your name is TOP GUN. You are on £50,000 a year, which is tidy, but the fact is that you are just DESPERATE FOR MORE MONEY. You need money - your partner, your car, all the rest of it. You want more money - and quick. Ideally you need another £20,000 to get you out of the hole that you're in right now.

Now - Top Gun, you're in the frame for a new job. The editor in chief, THE BOSS, is starting up a new tabloid. It's going to be pretty similar to the one you're already on. You have been earmarked to run the whole show. And not only would you love to do it, but you'd be pretty perfect for the job - you've been around the block a bit. You have all the skills. You'd be perfect.

It goes without saying that you'd like as much money as you can get for this post. You know there's going to be the small matter of a golden handshake - and boy do you need that. You'd take £20,000 but, obviously, if there's more on offer, then you'll take it.

Then there's the small matter of your salary. Well - you want this job, you'd happily take it for the same amount. But it's a big step up, and you reckon you might, at a pinch, be able to double your salary. Though realistically, you'd probably be happy with, say, £70,000 a year. Though, like with the golden handshake, you're looking to get as much loot as you can.

Now... there are some other minor matters. Owing to office politics, you're not actually going to be the editor of this new title. There's going to be an editor above you, in charge of two titles, and generally overseeing you. You will definitely be in charge of the whole show - but your actual title will be deputy editor. So... obviously you'd like to be the editor. It gets all the glory. The editor is the one with the power. But do you want to mess the whole deal up over this thing? How important is it to be the editor?

A car. Well there's probably going to be a car in it for you - and you'd like the biggest flashiest car you can get. Maybe you can get a real monster. See what you can get.

A secretary. You'd like a personal secretary - the more expensive the better.

Cheap secretaries come at £15,000 a year. You'd like a great one for £25,000.

The main thing is - you want this job. It's true that other media groups have been sniffing around - a glass of wine with some other boss. But you want this job and you want the money with it.

GOOD LUCK!

GAME 2 - THE FARMER'S DILEMMA

NOTES FOR THE HOT-SHOT LAWYER

Hello Mr Hot-Shot Lawyer you have got one hell of a problem on your hands. But not to worry - knowing your resourcefulness and animal cunning, you're bound to find a way through.

Here's what's happened: Your client, the Fat Tycoon, has shipped you down from Edinburgh to Southampton, and you are in one hell of a hurry. You've been flown down first class and you are going to meet THE FARMER. The Farmer has owned this little farm for quite a few years now. It's quite picturesque, really. Lovely views. A quaint little farmhouse. The perfect place for a summer's holiday. You have told the Farmer that you're down to see him on a "personal matter". But what could that be??

As per the map at the end, you can see what the farmer's got - quite a modest-sized farm of about 40 acres. He's got his little house with the back garden and front garden. In the home paddock is about 50 head of cattle. He likes his cattle. They're worth a bit.

There's also, as you can probably see, the marsh and the swamp. These are the little bits of his land in the valley beneath his farmhouse. The Swamp, as you can see, is right next to the main road.

Okay? Now - that's all by the by, because what you're really interested in is THE LANE. You probably can't even see it. The lane is a little lane running up to The Farmer's House. This is what you HAVE to buy. And the thing is, Hot-Shot Lawyer, you've only got one hour to do it.

So let me fill you in on the full picture. Your boss, The Fat Tycoon, has just managed to buy Neighbour 3's field. Can you see it?

The Fat Tycoon is looking to put a ton of houses on it. It's going to make him an absolute fortune. But can you see what the problem is? That's right - he's got no access to the land. The only way to get access to the land is up that little lane. That's why you've got to buy the lane.

There is another problem. The Fat Tycoon's biggest rival has just got hold of

Neighbour Number 2's field. And guess who will be shortly coming along to see the Farmer, but the rival's own lawyer. This lawyer will also be attempting to buy the lane. In fact... he's on his way over right this minute! So, along with having to charm the farmer, you are also facing massive time constraints. You only have ONE HOUR to sign that deal, otherwise the rival lawyer will have joined in the negotiations and you'll be in an auction. And believe me, if you get landed with an auction, then Mr Fat Tycoon is going to be GRAVELY DISAPPOINTED.

It goes without saying that your boss would prefer to pay as little as he can for the lane - but if push comes to shove, he'll go up to £50 million.

As for the rest of the farm - well, you've had the rest of the farm valued, and it's probably worth around £500,000. Maybe a bit more. Might be worth a lot more if you could put some housing on it. Perhaps. If you can get the farm as well as the lane, then you might even get a pay rise.

So, there you have it, Hot-Shot. Can you get the lane within the hour - and if so, for how little? All you need is the Farmer's signature on the back of this piece of paper, along with the amount he's sold it for. That will be all the confirmation you need. Happy? Well good luck - because if you don't come back with that lane, then somebody is going to be VERY, VERY UNHAPPY.... And remember now, you've only got ONE HOUR TO STRIKE THE DEAL, OTHERWISE YOU'VE SCREWED IT.

GAME 2 - THE FARMER'S DILEMMA

Hello Farmer! How we getting on? Enjoying life at your cosy little farmhouse, which you've owned for over thirty years? All those lovely views down across the valley and over the other side. Southampton may be only ten miles away, but your farm seems to be right in the very heart of the English countryside.

Now, take a good look at the map at the end - here's what you own. You own the house, the back garden, the garden, the home paddock, the marsh, the swamp and the lane. In all it's about 40 acres.

You've also got three Neighbours. Can you see their properties? That's Neighbours 1, 2 and 3. You don't know the owners. They left the area long ago. Neighbour 1's house is rented out, and as for Neighbours 2 and 3, their fields have also been rented out for well over a decade.

Got the picture? What a tranquil life you lead!

But actually... life's been getting a little hectic of late. You see, your eldest daughter, Clarissa, is getting married in a fortnight's time and you could really do with some money to pay for that wedding. See your garden on the map? That's where the marquee is going to be. The problem is, however, that you want to give Clarissa a really good send-off, and it's all gone a little bit over budget. In fact - by quite a lot. What you're looking at is a bill of around £30,000. Wow! You've got a week or two to pay it, but still... things aren't looking that great.

Perhaps, if the worst comes to worst, you could sell your cattle. You've got 50 head of prime cattle in the Home Paddock. You've had them for some years and are quite attached to them. But if you really needed to, you could sell the lot, and that should raise the necessary funds. And it's also true that perhaps you're ready to retire. So you'd rather keep the cattle - but if push came to shove, you'd sell them for your daughter's big day.

Now, something rather strange happened this morning. A Hot-Shot Lawyer called up just after breakfast. He's flying in to Southampton from Edinburgh, especially to see you. He's coming to speak to you on a "personal matter" - but what could that possibly be?

Well - it could be any number of things. But your hunch is that he could be wanting to buy the swamp. That's what you'd really like: sell him the Swamp. You've never much liked that ghastly mess anyway. Perhaps he might want to put some houses on it. Well if he wanted to do that, you'll be home and dry. If it's for housing, it might be worth a lot of money. You don't know how much. But it's bound to be a lot!

The farm, which you've recently had valued, is probably worth about £500,000 - and you don't really want to leave. You're very comfortable there. Maybe you'd sell for £750,000. Maybe you wouldn't. This whole business about property development - it's always so troublesome isn't it? You've never really bothered to get your head round it...

So anyway - now you've got your meeting with the Hot-Shot Lawyer. See what he's got to say. Maybe he'll want to buy something, maybe he won't...

I mean of course the money would be useful. But just remember now: you don't have to sell anything if you don't want to. If the going gets tough, you can always flog the cattle. But on the other hand, sometimes an offer can be just too good to refuse...

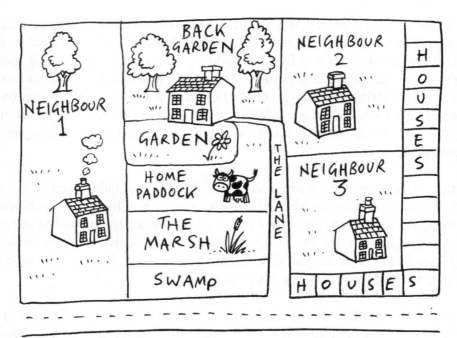

ON HOW TO NEGOTIATE...

I first gave these negotiating exercises to a team of a dozen reporters in Johannesburg. At the end of the second game, I said - "Well, team, what was the point of all that?"

Inge Liebenberg - star hack in the making - raised her hand.

"Yes Inge?"

"To make as much money as possible?"

I buried my head into my hands. Surprisingly, I did not construct these negotiating games in order to turn hacks into greedy grubbers who'll screw the mad-masters for every last penny. Not that that's necessarily a bad thing.

What I was hoping to get across was the importance of INFORMATION.

Whatever it is you're negotiating, then information is POWER.

Before you start negotiating, then you HAVE to do your homework beforehand. This is simply due diligence. If you're negotiating a pay rise, then find out what your peers are getting. Weigh up how important you are to the machine - are you a cog or just a piece of grease? Have you sounded out the rival papers? Is anyone else interested?

Just doing a little homework BEFORE you start negotiating will save you a lot of money. Might earn you another 10k a year - and that's simply because you've finally taken the trouble to find out what you're worth.

In the second negotiating game, with the farmer, I have had a lot of journalists selling the lane for BEANS. One reporter - dear Inge - got a THOUSANDTH of the price that Busisiwe reached. Inge sold the lane for £40,000; Busisiwe negotiated a fee of £40 MILLION.

What is going on here? NEVER get yourself into a negotiating situation if you have not done your homework.

That means that if you don't have enough information - like the Farmer in the second game - you should not be hustled into selling.

The very moment that somebody starts pressuring you into making a quick deal, then the alarm bells should start ringing. Put the brakes on. Take things easy. And above all, ask yourself if you have enough information or do you need some specialist advice?

At the very least, you can always tell the other negotiator - whether it's a lawyer or one of the mad-masters - that you need a day to think it over. Sleep on it. Do not be hustled into signing a deal the very moment that it has been presented to you.

One other mild detail. Since the essence of negotiating is about information, then it generally pays to keep your cards close to your chest. Just as you don't know what the mad-masters are going to offer, they also have no idea what size of salary would be acceptable to YOU.

Prospective mad-masters love to say, "Give me a ballpark figure," when negotiating a future salary - and a lot of hacks just completely cave in and give them that "ball-park figure". DON'T DO IT! By giving a ballpark figure, you have immediately put a cap on any future salary.

Much better to ask the prospective mad-master to give YOU a ballpark figure. This is done very politely. You say that you love the paper, you love the team - but please could HE name HIS ballpark figure. But get the question in FIRST. Stick it to the mad-masters before they stick it to you!

Negotiations are about delicately probing for information, whilst at the same time endeavouring not to give away too much. So if at all possible, try to get the other team to reveal their figure first. You could easily find that it is TRIPLE the figure that you initially had in mind. That is smart negotiating.

* Go in with as much information as possible.
* Once you're negotiating, be cautious about dispensing information to the other team.
* Are they pressuring you to sign? What do you have to lose by stalling?
* One last thing: as with all things pertaining to the Red Tops, always remain scrupulously polite. But that is what we are. We are charmers.

My final point from the first negotiating game. Do we think that having the title of "The Editor" is important? Does it make any odds - or is it just a bit of journalistic vanity?

In my book, the title of editor is CRUCIAL. As we all know, on any Red Top there will be about forty people who have the word "Editor" in their job title. But there can only be one person in charge. One person who gets the glory. One person who picks up all the awards. One person who's running the whole railway set. One person who is wined and dined by the Prime Minister at Chequers. And one person who has the superstars falling at their feet. That is THE EDITOR. And that is why, if you've got your heart set on becoming one of the mad-masters, then you've got to aim for the top job and nothing else. So - good luck my friend. You're going to need it!

Some say that being an editor is the most enthralling job in the world. It's certainly very lucrative. It can also open a lot of doors. But there's not much fun to be had. The fun is always out on the road. That's where the reporters are and that's where the action is.

I certainly know which job I'd prefer.

Any day of the week.

Paperbooks is part of the Legend Times Group alongside Legend Press, Legend Business, New Genearation Publishing and Write Connections. A recently relaunched non-fiction publisher, Paperbooks focuses on creating unique and creative books in a variety of genres. It's 2012 titles were in the fields of cookery and memoir, with a plan to extend this list in the coming years.

For information on all companies within the Legend Times Group,

come visit us at www.legendpress.co.uk

follow us @legend_press